Fast Track

For

Caregivers

A practical guide for managing care while preserving your sanity.

This book is available at discount when purchased in bulk
for premiums and sales promotions as well as for
fundraising or educational use.
For information, contact us at:
RosstrumPublishing@gmail.com.

While the authors have made every effort to provide accurate telephone numbers and Internet addresses at the time of publication, neither the publisher nor the authors assume any responsibility for errors or for changes that occur after publication. Further, the authors and publisher do not have any control over and do not assume any responsibility for third party websites or their content.

Library of Congress Control Number: 2008943279

Rosstrum Publishing™
The Rosses
8 Strawberry Bank Road
Suite 20
Nashua, New Hampshire 03062-2763

Manufactured in the United States of America

First printing, February 2009

1 3 5 7 9 10 8 6 4 2

Dedication

To Mom
who illustrated the need for this book

Acknowledgements

This book would not have been possible without the help and assistance of many people who have assured the integrity of the information contained herein.

The authors are grateful to Peter Ewing, Dr. Harris Faigel, Susan Frenette, Brian Hammar, Dr. Ed Jacobs, Karen Johnson, Mike Johnson, George Lambert, Matt Lewin, Essy Moverman, Edythe Pallin, Dale Phillips, Mindy Phillips, Louise Polley, Ted Pottel, Todd Savelle, Pat Beck Zambri, Bernie Ziegner, and the Tyngsborough Writers' Group.

In addition, many groups and agencies assisted by helping others as well as the authors. They have provided information and assistance to patients in our care and members of the public. All benefit from their caring. They include the New Hampshire Vocational Rehabilitation Commission and the Social Security Administration.

The assistance of these and others have been invaluable, whether offering criticism or acting as readers.

Any errors or omission belong entirely to the authors.

Fast Track

For

Caregivers

A practical guide for managing care while preserving your sanity.

By

Esther Ross

and

Joseph Ross

Table of Contents

About the Book

The authors designed this book as a reference. The reader is not expected to read it from cover to cover, as you would a novel. Use the sections as you need them.

We use several conventions in this book.

We means the authors. We have extensive backgrounds of over 40 years each in education, health, advocacy and in dealing with the problems and concerns we discuss.

This book is meant as a guide to help the caregiver negotiate the proper path through and within the system. We are neither doctors nor trained medical personnel. We are not trying to impart medical information. We are also not trying to give you instructions about how to adapt various devices. That is the responsibility of a Physical Therapist, Occupational Therapist or other professional. Do not use this book and its information as a substitute for proper medical advice or treatment. We encourage you at all times to consult with your doctors, dentists, pharmacists, therapists, and any other health care professionals.

Throughout the book, we use *him, her, he, she,* and *patient* interchangeably. Do not interpret *him* or *her* to mean a person of a specific gender. Professionals in all fields as well as caregivers can be and are both men and women. It is simply easier to use *him* or *her* instead of *him/her* or *he/she*.

When we refer to a *Doctor,* we mean a licensed medical practitioner. This book discusses a variety of caregivers, ranging from a medical doctor to nurse, occupational therapist, nurse practitioner, pharmacist or any other appropriate professional.

We use the term *caregiver* to mean you. While *caregiver* is a term which can normally mean any doctor, nurse, assistant or any other person providing service to a patient, we will try to avoid that term when referring to anyone except you.

There are many areas involved in caregiving. Some of the items discussed may apply to more than one area. They include: consideration and preparation prior to becoming a caregiver; caregiving in the patient's home; caring for a patient in *your* home; visiting and supervising actions within a nursing home, hospice or hospital; and actions after the death of your loved one.

Throughout the book, we will present illustrations. They are stories based on real events and real people. The names have been changed.

All of the references to web sites or telephone numbers were checked carefully immediately before publication. Any which could not be verified were eliminated. Despite that effort, web sites and phone numbers change from time to time and some organizations we have mentioned may no longer be operating. Please be assured that we have been as careful as possible.

We hope this book is valuable for you and makes your being a caregiver as rewarding and painless as possible. Good Luck.

The Authors

Introduction

We are all involved in it, some more than others. Some do it better than others. We start life as recipients of care. What a mother or father does is the first form of caregiving. Without much prior training, a parent provides the food, clothing, nurturing, and guidance every baby needs.

The focus of this book is to help the caregivers of those requiring care. The usual recipients are the elderly or younger people, often disabled or handicapped either physically or mentally.

According to a 1997 US Census Bureau report,[1] about nine million individuals require

---

[1] Census Brief (CENBR/97-5), US Department of Commerce, Economics and Statistics

personal assistance to carry out everyday activities. About half of the primary caregivers live with the patient.

When unprepared, becoming a caregiver can be a daunting experience. However, in addition to helping a loved one, you will also learn a great deal about yourself, the healthcare system, and other people.

Success in your endeavor is measured in different terms than what you may be used to. The bar measuring that success is raised or lowered as you go along. At various times, you will have clear choices, no choices, and gray areas, where you need to make compromises. Traveling down the caregiver road will allow you to recognize your skills, your flaws, and your limitations. Being a caregiver can be your most difficult experience, and yet your most rewarding one.

This book was written so that the ordinary person can navigate through an extraordinary system. You will learn to learn the system.

The book is divided into several sections:

Section I - Early Considerations (beginning on page 1). In assuming the role, you will learn the steps to take *before* you assume the task of becoming a caregiver. We will discuss whether or not you should be a caregiver at all. Many of these steps should be taken before the *need* for a caregiver arises, whether or not you are or are going to be that caregiver. You should also consider that it is likely that your role will change as the patient progresses from requiring only out-patient services to needing the more extensive care which can only be given on an in-patient basis.

Section II - Out-patient Care (beginning on page 19). The next section deals with working either in the patient's home or in your

_____

Administration, Bureau of the Census, December 1997.

home. It may involve the coordination of care by outside agencies or professionals, but on an out-patient basis.

Section III - In-patient care (beginning on page 97). A completely different set of rules governs the caregiver's actions when considering "in-patient" circumstances, whether in a hospital, nursing home, hospice or rehabilitation facility.

Section IV - After Death (beginning on page 119). In the next section, we will consider the caregiver's rights, responsibilities, and responses after the patient passes away.

Section V - Questions and Answers (beginning on page 139). In this section, we will address some of the questions which occur often. All of the questions concern material which is covered in more detail in earlier sections.

In all instances, we will lead the caregiver through the system. One of the biggest problems caregivers are faced with is the inability to obtain correct answers. A big part of that problem is not knowing the right questions. This book will help.

Fast Track

For

Caregivers

Section I - Early Considerations

Years ago, families lived together and took care of each other. Today, people live longer, but not necessarily better. Health insurance coverage and those costs associated with caring for a sick patient all-too-often govern the type and extent of care a patient receives, but that's not the way it should be. A major addition to stress occurs when legitimate claims are denied by insurance carriers, despite the presence of appropriate coverage. Some of those denials result in court action. Others result in complaints to government agencies. Even if claims are ultimately paid, these events lead to frustration and high stress levels. We appreciate the integrity of those companies who process claims correctly and pay legitimate bills in a timely manner, but cannot forget that some companies think it is more cost effective to keep denying claims.

They prefer to pay fewer claims with the extra costs associated with them, while saving more money because of those who do not follow through on the available appeals. Unscrupulous companies use the advantage of time to wait until many policy holders give up and stop pursuing payment.

There are major considerations about the choice of whether you should become a caregiver. The duties of finance and time are significant. Regardless of the amount of insurance, there are always costs associated with taking care of a loved one, above and beyond that which is covered. No matter how much we try, there are only twenty-four hours into a day. In addition to maintaining a job (sometimes two or three jobs), family responsibilities need to be considered. They often include shopping and cleaning, as well as monitoring the medical care of the family. Frequent medical appointments and other patient care tasks may mean time lost from work. Doctors are often late for appointments and there is invariably waiting time if tests are required.

In-patient therapy or confinement adds the additional responsibility of shopping for the best facility in a particular circumstance. Sometimes, there are no local beds available or local facilities can't manage the patient properly, so out-of-town or even out-of-state travel or transfer may be necessary.

Not every person can be an appropriate caregiver. You should assess your own stress threshold, your ability to handle multiple tasks, your own health and well being, your family's health and well being, and your ability to survive with sleep interruptions.

An Illustration

Brian[2] visited his mother on the way home from his second job. After the visit, a friend suggested they go to dinner at the local Chinese restaurant to relieve the stress and provide a needed break. After dinner, Brian put the leftovers in his refrigerator and prepared to visit his mother again the next day. Try as he might, he could not find the keys to his car. After looking "everywhere," he decided to retrace his steps. He found the keys right where he left them, in the refrigerator next to the leftovers. He was concerned that the loss of items was becoming more and more frequent.

Stress will affect each of us in different ways.

Before you agree to become a caregiver, you should understand that some family members and close friends are likely to resist your ideas and try to tell you what to do. You should listen to their thoughts and opinions even if they appear silly. Sometimes, the ideas of others will turn out to be valuable. You should weigh the plusses and minuses, but remember the final decision is yours. Other people are trying to be helpful because they care about the patient, as you do.

Be prepared to experience strong feelings. Some will be the positive feelings of helping a loved one and making a difference. You need to be aware of the negative ramifications:

- A sense of isolation
- Huge responsibility
- Worry about the quality of care
- Guilt at not doing enough (real or imagined)

---

[2] Although the stories are based on fact, the names and some details have been changed.

- Resentment toward the patient
- Resentment toward family and friends
- Resentment from family members
- Loss of time with your own family
- Concern over your ability to maintain the level of care
- Concern over your ability to get help where needed
- Fatigue
- Guilt at the loss of ability by the patient despite your best efforts
- Loss of sleep
- Loss of energy

On some occasions, you need to draw a line. You must assure the friend or family member that care is being managed by a competent physician or other professionals and that you are in constant contact with that professional. Sometimes, you will need to put some distance between you and the other party so you do not become upset.

In many cases, the most resistant person to your becoming the caregiver is the patient. Most people, especially the elderly, do not want to give up their freedom. If you need to take the car away from an elderly person, be ready for an argument. The patient will often try to bargain. "I'll keep driving, but I won't drive at night." Resist that argument.

An Illustration

Corrine, 87 years-old, owned a six year old car. Despite it's age, the car had only 28,000 miles on it. Corrine refused to give it up despite the fact that her daughter told her that it would be less expensive to take a cab everywhere she went. On a trip to the local supermarket, Corrine was involved in an accident in which her car collided with another car while heading toward the exit. There was a long discussion trying to assess fault, but Corrine insisted that she did not see the other car, which was "speeding" toward the same exit. It was obvious to her daughter that Corrine should not be driving because her reflexes, judgment, and eyesight were all diminished. After a discussion with the local police, her daughter finally insisted that Corrine no longer drive and took the keys.

Once the decision is made, you must be insistent.

As they face illness, financial difficulties, or aging, some patients begin to make poor decisions. This may be a normal attempt to retain independence. When you have concerns, you need to take action. Consult with the patient's attorney, physician, social worker, or other professional who may be familiar with the situation. Sometimes, taking over is the only viable option to prolong life.

Use a Checklist

Generally, the first steps for a prospective caregiver occur long before the need arises. If you feel that you will be a caregiver either in your home or in the patient's home, there are many things to check. Keep in mind that elderly patients will generally progress from in-home care to a separate facility. Focus first on what you need to do for care in your home or the patient's home. This list will help you decide if in-home caregiving is appropriate for the patient and if you should be that caregiver. If you plan to keep the patient in your home, some items will not need to be considered. Use these questions for at-home care as soon as possible and before it becomes necessary:

- Is the home warm?

   This may not matter now, but you need to know that the furnace is in proper working order. As part of this review, you should have the emergency number for the repair person posted near the furnace and on the refrigerator door, in sight of the patient and caregiver.

- Does the tank have fuel, if required?

If the tank is full, that is an indication that the patient either has a contract or remains aware of the need or that they are not turning on the heat. The emergency number of the fuel supplier should also be posted near the furnace and on the refrigerator door.

- Is there hot water?

All parts of the heating system need to work correctly. Check the water temperature to be sure it is safe. Frail and elderly people have more sensitive skin and can burn easily.

- Is the plumbing working?

Plumbing includes all sinks, bathtub, shower, toilet, drains and faucets.

- Are the locks working and are they sufficient?

This is an area which can easily be ignored, especially by the elderly. Also make sure you have keys to all the locks.

- Is the telephone working?

Necessary even if you generally use a cell phone. If you do use a cell, make sure there is a charger and it is being used.

- Is the air conditioning working?

This can be a critical issue if the patient has any lung or breathing problems, or other health impairments.

- Have the filters been cleaned or changed?

This is the most neglected task in most households.

- Are housekeeping tasks being done?

Lack of cleanliness can be sign of increasing difficulties, where the patient loses the ability to perform even minimal tasks.

- Are smoke and carbon monoxide detectors working?

If there are other detectors, they should also be checked at the same time. This may involve a step as simple as changing a battery.

- Is the vehicle, if any, in good working order?

Are the tires inflated properly? Has an oil change been done on schedule? Also consider the mechanical condition of the auto as a whole.

- Is there enough food on the premises and is it appropriate?

This is another area where patients can be neglectful. Food also means fluids. The importance of juices, fruit, vegetables and water cannot be underestimated. Don't neglect variety. One of the more versatile foods is wild salmon. It can be grilled, baked, poached, or even made in the microwave. Two great benefits of salmon are the high level of omega-3 fatty acids (good for the heart) and the softness of the fillet (good for those who can't chew). This is only one of a number of foods which are appropriate for the elderly or for others who have difficulty chewing. You also should check on the expiration dates of everything in the refrigerator and pantry. Old or spoiled food can be a sign of forgetting. The elderly often forget to throw out spoiled food because their sense of smell has diminished.

- Is the patient properly oriented?

You should know if the patient understands the date, time and place.

- How is the patient's mental state?

Can you cope with a person who is depressed, forgetful, or confused?

- Is the patient clean and well groomed?

As the caregiver, you may be required to keep the patient clean and dressed.

- Is the patient's weight reasonable?

In addition to the health considerations of excess weight, you may be required to lift, move, or support the patient. This may cause problems for anyone who has not been properly trained or has health issues. On the other hand, if the patient has a weight which is too low, it could be a sign that she is not eating enough.

- How are the patient's motor skills?

If a person has proper motor skills, she will be able to open bottles, doors, shower knobs and curtains, cut food properly, sign checks, and phone for help.

- Is the patient independent?

Before the need for a caretaker is apparent, is the patient capable of paying his own bills? If not, you may be required to cope with a number of problems in the course of normal care. These may include late or missing payments, dunning notices, or utility shutoff notices.

- Are there any pets?

If the patient has pets, you should make sure you can take care of the pet as well as the patient. This will include food, cleaning, even vet bills.

- Is medical care under control?

There are several components to medical care. They involve whether or not the patient is having regular visits to a doctor. Medications need to be arranged in such a way that they are taken on time and in the correct dosages. They also need to be checked to be sure that they have not expired. Any upcoming medical appointments should be easily tracked.

- Is there a calendar to track medical appointments?

There should also be a chart indicating when each medication should be taken.

Calendars belong on the refrigerator (see the next item).

- Is the refrigerator being used properly on the outside?

The refrigerator is generally the best bulletin board in the home. In case of emergencies, there should be a complete and up to date list of all medications and their doses. Important phone numbers should also be posted. Other health information should be posted so that emergency personnel can find it easily.

- Is anyone checking on the patient regularly?

If a neighbor or friend stops by regularly, this might even provide some respite care for you if you are the caregiver.

- Can you listen to your patient and determine truth from fiction?

Some patients find it difficult to remember events correctly and accurately.

In addition to helping you determine your ability to become a caregiver, this list will also help the patient to maintain his home. If you take care of these items, the patient may remain independent for a longer period of time.

An Illustration

Amy was in the Alzheimer's unit of a nursing home. When her daughter arrived to visit, Amy mentioned that the doctor had come to see her and had played music, just for her. The daughter did not believe the story. Later, while at the nursing station, a nurse mentioned that the doctor had, indeed, played the piano for Amy.

It is sometimes difficult to tell truth from fiction. You must not only listen, you need to know the correct questions. You also need to know whom to ask for both the daily little questions and also the bigger questions about care. This book will teach you the questions.

The Language Barrier

Many doctors speak in "doctorspeak." They are not trying to confuse you. It is an attempt to be accurate, not to hide the meaning of what they tell you. However, those of us who do not speak the language often have difficulty understanding. This is more of a problem when you need to make a decision. Most decisions can be made the next day. In cases where an immediate decision is required, ask the doctor to explain the problem in layman's terms along with the options, the pros and cons and the risks.

When the doctor explains his diagnosis, the options available, the medication to be used, and any other information, write it down. When a caregiver considers choices later or the next day, it is easy to forget half of what you were told or you may recall just enough of the explanation for your choices to be wrong.

If there are terms you do not understand, and if you have computer access, go to one of the online medical dictionaries. Start with Medline Plus (http://medlineplus.gov and click on "dictionary"). Although not the only site available, this site, run by the National Institutes of Health, has more links to other resources than others we have seen.

Become Informed

As a caregiver, you will make decisions about everything from meals to medicine. No one expects you to be an expert. The most important advantage you can have is to know where to look and what to ask. A good place to start is with Medline Plus (http: //medlineplus.gov).[3] This site can supply you with many resources. Included are links to health topics, drugs, news, directories of doctors and facilities, a medical encyclopedia, and a medical dictionary. Before you say *yes* or *no* to any procedure, you must do the homework. Do not let anyone tell you they know what is best for the patient.[4] If necessary, get a second opinion or even a third opinion.

An Illustration

Armando had a bedside emergency while in the nursing home. The nursing home staff told Armando's daughter to take him to the hospital, citing that they did not want to call an ambulance and that there might be no insurance coverage. His daughter immediately called 9-1-1 for an ambulance. During the transport, Armando developed another problem but the EMTs were able to stabilize him, saving his life.

Sometimes, there is no time for a second opinion and you need to exercise your own best judgment.

If you want a second opinion and there is time, ask your doctor to send the records to the doctor giving the second opinion. Therefore, tests may not need to be repeated. (If the doctor refuses to send records for a second opinion, find another doctor.) Good doctors will

---

[3] Medline Plus is a service of the U.S. National Library of medicine and the National Institutes of Health.

[4] Some of the information contained in this section is taken from *Five Steps to Safer Health Care.* Patient Fact Sheet, published by the Agency for Healthcare Research and Quality, Rockville, MD. AHRQ Publication Number 04-M005, February, 2004. (http://www.ahrq.gov/consumer/5steps.htm)

encourage you to get a second opinion so that you feel comfortable with what is to come. Before you take the patient to the second doctor, call to be sure they have received the records. It may also be a good idea to carry the records yourself. If you hand carry those documents, you are sure they are received by the second doctor. At that appointment, tell the second professional everything you have told the first and add the information the first doctor told you. If the two doctors disagree and you still feel uncomfortable, ask for a third opinion, either from both doctors or by contacting the appropriate group within the specialty you need. The on-line directories for most specialties offer a **Locate a doctor in your area** section. Most insurance companies, as well as Medicare, will pay for second opinions.

No professional should assume you are able to make a decision on the spot about anything important. It is the professional's job to give you not only all the information you need, but also all the information you want. All of your questions should be answered to your satisfaction. You always have the ability to keep asking questions, and if necessary, find someone who will answer your questions. Sometimes, you may even elect to change providers.

An Illustration

Ken was a 14-year old with an impacted wisdom tooth. He also had a medical condition in which he would react to stress by breaking out in a sweat and would become physically ill. His mother indicated to the oral surgeon that Ken needed to be given something to keep him calm and that the room air conditioner needed to be set very cool. The surgeon replied, "I'm the doctor here. I'll determine what he needs."

Ken's mother immediately told Ken to get out of the chair. They left the office and went to a hospital-based oral surgeon who spent the time getting to know Ken and medicated him properly before the operation.

While it is true that you must listen to the doctor, the doctor must also listen to you.

Do not let anyone rush you into a decision. Examine all the options carefully and consider what is best for the patient. If you feel it is appropriate, consult with family, friends, and those who may have experienced the same problem. They may have good questions to be asked.

Another part of being informed is making sure the professionals are informed. You must have a list of all medications for doctors and pharmacists, including over-the-counter preparations, homeopathic preparations and vitamins. In addition, bring a complete list of allergies experienced by the patient, even if it does not seem important. Then, if the patient needs another medication or a surgical procedure, the doctor will know what medications to prescribe and what cross reactions may occur. In the case of surgery, many procedures cannot be done if the patient was taking aspirin or other medications which affect blood (because aspirin is a blood thinner and can cause unwanted bleeding).

Some facilities and professionals erect a barrier that hinders you from getting information. This is given under the guise of patient privacy. Under the HIPAA[5] rules, a facility has the responsibility of maintaining privacy. You will encounter instances where people and facilities may not want to share information with you about the patient. That is

---

[5] Health Insurance Portability and Accountability Act of 1996.

why it is important for you to have a current Power of Attorney and Health Care Proxy, giving you both the authority to be informed and the authority to act on behalf of the patient. Be prepared to have the facility argue with you about releasing information. You must be persistent at all times.

Choose Quality

The most important decisions you need to make involve quality; quality health plans, quality hospital and other facilities, quality doctors.

The health plans include Medicare providers both for care and for prescriptions.

If you are in a position to select a plan, consider what is important to you. The plan should:

- Cover the doctors you want
- Cover the hospitals you want
- Provide the covered services you need when you need them
- Have a history of doing a good job without a constant need to fight and appeal
- Have high ratings by its members especially in areas of your concerns

When looking for either a primary doctor or a specialist, consider:

- Certifications in the field
- Training and experience
- Ratings from other patients (in a strange or new area, have a talk with some nurses at the local hospitals)
- The doctor's willingness to discuss treatments and options and to listen to your concerns and points of view

Any hospital or other facility should be accredited by the appropriate agency. The facility should:

- Be rated highly by your state, consumer groups, and other organizations
- Have significant experience in whatever condition your patient has
- Have a monitoring program in place to insure and improve the quality of care
- Provide a level of care which will meet your patient's needs

Grandparents - A Special Case

Grandparents can be considered as caregivers and as patient. On the one hand, grandparents can become the caregivers for very young children. On the other hand, grandparents often become the recipient of caregiving. There are special considerations in both cases.

Grandparents as caregivers

If you, as grandparents, are considering becoming the caregivers for infant children, the most important consideration is stamina. Face it, you are not as young as you once were. Chasing a toddler around the house is a big task and you need to be in condition to assume 24 hour care.

Unfortunately today, nearly 1 1/2 million grandparents are raising young children for a variety of reasons:[6] the biological parents may have health, alcohol, and/or drug abuse problems or financial difficulties; the child may have disabilities or special needs which the parents are not able to address; or the child may have been abandoned or neglected. This

---

[6] According to research done in 2000 by Rand Corporation under a grant from the National Institute for Child Health and Human Development.

number does not include those where children, parents, and grandparents share a household.

When considering whether or not to become the caregiver for an infant, try to consider your resources, not just the obvious emotional bond.

An Illustration

Umberto became the caregiver of his young grandchild. After time passed, Umberto complained of lower back problems and general aches and pains. He went to his physician, who discovered that Umberto's pain was the result of continually lifting his grandchild in and out of the crib, car seat, and shopping carts.

Monitor your own health and abilities. Lifting a 25 pound toddler is still lifting 25 pounds.

Think about the legal issues. You need a **Power of Attorney** in case of emergencies. If you don't have one, a hospital or doctor may refuse to treat the baby. You may need legal custody for the same reason. The last thing to consider is adoption if the baby's parents are not around or are permanently incapable of caring for their child.

Explore your **health insurance** program. Some policies have conditions, waiting times and exclusions as well as deductibles and co-payments. A policy may have a limit on services, either by the number of visits allowed for a particular condition or the amount of money which may be paid. Sometimes, grandchildren can be added to an existing policy; sometimes, not. If the child has special needs, it is even more important to read the fine print of the policy.

Consider whether the child has **special needs**. It is even more difficult to care for a handicapped child. Caring for a sick or handicapped child often requires additional help. Check with various community and state agencies to locate service providers, funding, or other assistance as required. You will need the Power of Attorney or legal guardianship before you start this search.

Grandparents as patients

At some point, it will become obvious that your parent or grandparent can no longer be on his own. Despite his insistence that he is still perfectly capable, he is not. The question to answer is, "Are you the appropriate caregiver?" Will your siblings, children, or friends of the patient help and support your decision? You can't do it alone, especially if the patient is to remain in his own home. In fact, that might not be the best placement.

An Illustration

Darlene always arrived at her mother's home at 7:00 a.m. to help with her mother's shower. One morning, Darlene was caught in traffic and called her mother to tell her NOT to take her shower alone. Afraid that Darlene would be late to work, Darlene's Mother attempted to shower herself. Unsteady, she slipped, fractured her hip, and broke an arm. Darlene discovered her mother an hour later.

Not every patient is capable of exercising good judgment.

The first job is to determine the best degree of intervention. Can the elderly patient live alone or will he need to be in your home? Another piece of this puzzle involves whether the patient will not be able to return to his own home, or if the patient suffered an accident from which he can recover enough. Also consider if either home is appropriate or if an in-patient arrangement like a nursing home, hospital, hospice, or assisted-living facility is necessary. Do not be afraid to involve professionals in this determination.

You should meet with your siblings and others who may be involved in the care of your loved one. The first job is to determine if you are the best choice as caregiver. If so, explain the need for assistance from others. Also, make certain that there will be no arguments when you determine that a particular action is necessary. A predetermined tie-breaker person might be needed. You do not want to be in the middle of an argument every time you make a decision.

After all of these considerations and discussions, you should be ready to decide if you are the appropriate caregiver, that you are up to the task ahead. If not, someone else might be a better choice to care for the needs of the patient.

Section II - Out-Patient Care

The Setting

Now that you are a caregiver, where do you start?

Start with the physical layout of your house (or the patient's house). If the house needs some changes so that the patient can get around better, seek professional help and guidance. A licensed carpenter, plumber, nurse, physical therapist, occupational therapist or the patient's doctor can guide you. Keep in mind that the patient may need some training on equipment you buy or add to the house. Also keep in mind that, if you add equipment, you should review your insurance coverage. You may need to increase the policy limits on your contents.

Documents

Keep all the paperwork for the patient in one central location. You must be able to find what you need quickly and easily when you apply for benefits. The Social Security Administration, either for regular benefits or for disability benefits, requires certain documents. So do local, state and Federal agencies providing everything from Medicare to Medicaid, from respite care to free rides or reduced cost items. Having papers in one central location will help you work with the system. Do not give an original document to anyone. Always send copies of any document which is requested. The Social Security Administration is the exception. They require originals of certain documents but will copy them and return the originals to you.

Among the items you should have are:

- Durable Power of Attorney (Keep in mind that a Power of Attorney ends with the death of the patient. To continue acting on behalf of the patient, you will also need to be the executor of the estate, even if there is no estate to speak of.)
- Living Will or Advanced Medical Directive
- A will
- Birth certificate
- Marriage certificate, if married or applying for widow's benefits
- Naturalization papers, if applicable
- All life insurance policies (They will also show cash value as well as death benefits.)
- Any private health insurance plans
- Homeowners or renters insurance policy
- Deeds to any real estate
- Most recent property tax bill

- Most recent mortgage bill or statement, or rent receipt
- Trust documents
- Financial account information, including checking accounts, savings accounts, IRA statements, annuity statements, credit cards, stocks, and bonds (Keep statements going back at least 36 months.[7])
- An explanation of any large deposits or withdrawals (involving $2,000 or more) - This is also needed for some forms of assistance.
- Social Security benefit statement for both patient and spouse, if either is collecting
- Earning statements for any other sources of income
- Social Security card
- Medicare and any other health insurance cards
- Passport
- Information on any lawsuits
- Listing of contents in any safe deposit box
- Location or control of safe deposit box keys
- Automobile title and registration (Also keep a note of the current mileage.)
- Prepaid burial or funeral contracts
- Income tax returns for the previous three years

Emergency Equipment

A most important device is an emergency response button. Every patient should have one whether he lives alone or with you. There

---

[7] This is needed if applying for many assistance programs.

are times you will need to be away from the patient, for a number of reasons. A patient can slip and fall, have breathing problems, or have other concerns which require an emergency call. There are a number of companies that provide emergency notification and assistance. Some also keep medical records on file in case a doctor needs information in a hurry. A list can be found in Appendix A (see page 161).

An Illustration

Frank wore a bracelet with an emergency button and was quick to tell everyone he always used it. However, he took the bracelet off when he showered. During one shower, he slipped and fell. He was not able to get up or reach the bracelet. His daughter found him in the tub more than an hour later.

The bracelet does no good if the patient does not wear it. Make sure it is waterproof or kept nearby.

When you are researching companies, keep several points in mind:
- If you are paying a monthly fee, some companies will not also charge for equipment
- The company you choose should help you set it up, even if that is only over the phone
- Don't sign a long term contract (You should be able to change companies if you want to and you should be able to cancel without any penalties.)
- If the patient does any international traveling, ask the companies if the button works in that foreign country, or if they have a company they work with - Ask if a different base unit will be required, if there is any additional cost,

and how far ahead you should tell them about the trip

- Price is important, but it is not everything (See if there are other features you like.)
- Make sure you know if batteries need to be replaced and if there is any automatic notice from the company about when batteries should wear out
- When you select a company and receive the equipment, test it to be sure it is working properly (When you test, tell the operator immediately that you are testing only and that there is no emergency.)
- Ask how often you should test the system (Ask the company if they call you on a regular schedule to either check the system or remind you to check it. You should also test anytime you move any of the equipment.[8])

Other Equipment

An Illustration

Ellen was told to buy a cane for help in walking and to help her keep her balance. She purchased the cane at the local drug store. After using the cane for several months, Ellen began to develop hip and back pain. The cup (the rubber piece at the bottom of the cane) was worn. Also, the length of the cane was never properly set for her height.

---

[8] Moving the equipment involves unplugging the base unit and moving it to a different electrical outlet and/or plugging the phone connection into a different jack.

The problem could have been avoided if Ellen consulted a therapist or her doctor before using the cane.

Every piece of equipment should be checked regularly for wear and tear. For example, a wheelchair's tires can wear out, making it more difficult to push the chair. When the tires are worn, the brakes will not work well because wheelchair brakes work by exerting pressure against the tire.

Before buying anything or having any work done, consult with the doctor, get a prescription, and talk to the insurance company. Some policies will pay for all or some of these items when you can show that they are needed.

When you talk to insurance companies, the words you must use are "medically necessary."[9]

Some patients require oxygen. If the patient can get around, even sometimes, ask for a portable tank, in addition to the large one in the home. This piece of equipment can be carried like a purse and allows a patient to go almost anywhere (except on an airplane where special rules apply, often at very high cost). For trips which will take longer than the several hours of oxygen provided in a tank, most companies can lend you an extra tank. If the patient will be away from home for a longer period, the oxygen company can arrange for another branch or even another company to make sure that the patient's oxygen supply is not interrupted. If the patient is planning to fly, oxygen concentrators are generally the only things that can be used, and only specific brands are approved by the Federal Aviation Administration. If your present company

---

[9] Insurance companies and social service agencies react to catch phrases. You should always use these terms when writing or speaking with those organizations.

cannot supply one, there are many companies specializing in those rentals.

For the home, the companies will supply a larger tank. First, make sure the company offers service on a regular basis. Company workers should refill the tank without your having to keep track. Every time they come, the worker should check to be sure the tank is working correctly. Ask for an extra long tube. The company can supply a tube long enough to allow the patient to go almost anywhere in the house. Do not allow smoking anywhere oxygen is kept. If there are disposable units, have the company discard them. Throwing them in a dumpster can lead to potentially deadly results.

Since you are the caregiver, it is fair to assume that you will need to drive the patient in your car, either for tests, doctor appointments, shopping, or for pleasure. In any case you should have a state-issued handicapped decal so you can park in specially designated spots close to the door of a facility. You will need proper documentation proving that the patient is handicapped, has trouble walking or breathing, or otherwise qualifies. The form is sometimes available on line. Go to your state's web site and follow the links to the motor vehicle department. In any case, the patient's doctor will need to complete part of the form. The rules allow you to use the decal only when the patient is in the car. If you park at a meter, do not put in any coins. Handicapped parking is free at any meter.

If the patient is using a walker, there are some steps to make it easier. The therapist should supply tennis balls (not covered by insurance). Tennis balls on the non-wheel legs make it easier to move the walker smoothly. If the therapist does not supply them, spend the money yourself but ask the therapist to put them on properly. Tennis balls are not expensive.

One of the problems with assistive technology is learning and knowing about what is available. One Federally-funded project, AbleData, has an extensive list of resources. They can be reached at www.abledata.com or at 1-800-227-0216.

Comfort Items.

Some equipment is not insurance related. These items are used for **comfort** or to make life easier. The number and variety of items is virtually unlimited. There are items which offer assistance, from support for body parts to blankets (when feet are sensitive), purifiers, large button controls, pill cutters and organizers, long handled shoehorns, portable and temporary hardware. If the television picture is too small for a patient, there are magnifying screens available which go over the television screen and enlarge the viewing area. You can also purchase a magnifying glass, with or without a light, which will make it easier to read the newspaper or any documents.

Do not strain your **hearing** because a patient needs the television or radio louder than you are used to. A relatively inexpensive device can play the sound through a set of earphones which the patient can wear. The patient can then adjust the volume to any setting desired.

Even the **telephone** can be adapted for the hard of hearing. Call or visit your local electronics store for assistance, or call a medical supply house or other company specializing in hearing devices.

The items mentioned in this section are useful when the patient refuses to consider hearing aids. If the choice is hearing aids, ask if you should consider getting two. Natural sound comes through both ears, not just one. The use of two in some cases also adds to our ability to tell where the speaker is, in relation to the patient.

Many books and magazines are available in **large print** editions. Some **books** are also available **on tape**. Don't be afraid to ask. Most magazines and publishers have web sites and they will be happy to answer your questions. Also, do not forget the local library. Most have a selection of both books on tape and large print editions. Whether they do or not, consult the library. Librarians are usually knowledgeable people and are always willing to help. Other resources include many of the organizations founded to help blind or deaf people. These can be found in Appendix B (page 164).

In addition to the more sedentary comfort items are activities of a more exciting nature. A survey of more than 3,000 men and women[10] found that 73% of those between the ages of 57 and 64 and more than one-quarter of those between 75 and 85 continued to engage in sexual activity. Be aware that even handicapped patients may continue to engage in sexual relations.

Pets

Some of the most therapeutic comfort items are pets. Pets offer friendship, companionship and love. We cannot ignore the soothing effect of a pet. The pet will also make the patient feel more at home.

There is also a category called **working pets**, mostly dogs. These are animals trained to be working members of a household. They will even warn a patient and provide assistance during seizures. They can assist patients with balance problems, mobility problems, hearing problems or even psychiatric disabilities. By

---

[10] Inglis, Dr. Alan © 2004-2006 by www.healthrevelations.com

law, these pets are always allowed on buses, trains, in restaurants and many other facilities. A working animal list can be found in Appendix C (page 166).

Insurance

As the caretaker, either in your home or the patient's, you need to check the insurance coverage. If the patient has moved in with you, do not let her drive your car, if she is still capable of driving, unless you have added her as a driver on your auto insurance policy. A driver living in your household, but not listed on the policy may not be covered in case of an accident.

Your homeowners or tenants policy should also be checked. Your agent can help make sure you have enough coverage, not only for the patient, but also for other people who will come to your house, such as nurses, health aides, therapists, or social workers. If anyone slips and falls, whether or not it is your fault, you may be sued. If there is expensive equipment as the result of the patient's needs, you should consider adding those items to your policy. A room or area set aside to complete the extra paperwork can be covered with the low cost addition of an *incidental office* rider.

Medicare - What Everyone Should Know

There are several parts to Medicare. Medicare is a government sponsored health insurance program for those who are at least 65, younger than 65 but with certain disabilities, or at any age with end stage renal disease (permanent kidney failure requiring dialysis or a transplant). Applications can be made on-line, in person, or by phone (www.medicare.gov or 1-800-MEDICARE). Any information which is required can be sent in afterward. The counselors are well-trained and helpful. The information contained in this section is only an overview. For specific information about your case, consult Medicare directly.

Part A - The basic plan

Medicare Part A covers a portion of in-patient hospital care or care in skilled nursing facilities. It will also help with hospice and home health care if the patient meets certain criteria. Most people who have held a job will be eligible for Part A with no premium.

Covered items include blood when received as an in-patient; reasonable and necessary home health care, including nursing and health aide services, occupational therapy, physical therapy, and speech pathology; medical social services; durable medical equipment; and some medical supplies for home use.

Also covered is **hospice care** when the patient's life expectancy is six months or less. This includes drugs used to control symptoms and relieve pain.

During periods of confinement **in a hospital**, Part A will cover a semi-private hospital room, meals, hospital services and supplies. A private room will be covered only if the doctor orders it as medically necessary. Usually, prescriptions, other than an IV, are not covered.

In a **skilled nursing facility**, Part A will cover a semi-private room, meals, skilled nursing care, rehabilitative services, and supplies. To take advantage of this provision, the patient must have been in a hospital for at least three consecutive days for the same illness or condition.

Most Part A services are subject to deductibles and co-payments. These can be paid by other programs. We will discuss them later in this section.

Part B - Paying for the extras: Just Do It

Part B is an **optional program you should always take**. It covers doctors' services, out-patient care, some preventive care, some home health care, emergency room visits, and other medical services not covered by Part A. If the patient is applying for Medicare for the first time, she should also apply for Part B at the same time. Failure to do so will result in a higher premium when Part B is added.

Covered are **tests and services used to diagnose or treat** an illness or condition. As with all insurance, the service must be deemed "medically necessary." Second opinions, sometimes third opinions, may be covered for non-emergency surgery. Some smoking cessation programs may also be covered, with restrictions. Should the need arise, ask about coverage for programs involving drug and alcohol abuse.

Also covered are some items to prevent illness, like exams and lab tests, including blood tests, urinalysis, x-rays, MRIs, CAT scans, EKGs, yearly flu shots, pneumonia vaccines and other screening tests. Part B also covers ambulance services, blood other than what is covered by Part A, bone mass measurements (every two years to see if you are at risk for fractures), cholesterol, lipid, and triglyceride tests every five years, some chiropractic services, and even some clinical trials. Women are covered every year for a mammography and either yearly or every two years for a pap smear. Men are covered for a yearly PSA test (to help detect prostate cancer). There are limitations for outpatient mental health services, but there is some coverage.

Cancer screening tests are covered according to different schedules. Some restrictions are based on age, others on the spacing of time between tests and the patient's susceptibility.

Diabetes screening is also covered. If you have diabetes, some self-help training is covered. The testing supplies are also covered, although insulin is only covered if you have a prescription plan. Diabetics are also covered (as are those with renal failure) for medical nutrition therapy.

Eye exams, not usually covered, are included for diabetics, but only once every 12 months and only to check for diabetic retinopathy. When normal eye exams are included at the same time, that portion of the charge is not covered. If you have surgery because of a cataract in one or both eyes, and if an artificial lens is implanted (permanent, not a contact lens you insert and remove), one pair of glasses with standard frames is covered. A yearly glaucoma test is covered for those considered high risk.

Foot exams and treatment are included if you have diabetes related nerve damage and meet certain other conditions. Normal foot care, like nail trimming, is not covered.

Transplants may be covered, if the patient meets all the conditions. If coverage is provided, anti-rejection drugs are also covered.

Oxygen, wheelchairs, walkers, and hospital beds are among the covered **durable medical items**. Prosthetic items are also covered. These include artificial limbs, various braces, and internal supplies (like ostomy bags).

Hearing and balance exams are covered, but hearing aids are not.

If the patient is at high risk for **Hepatitis B**, the three shots required are covered.

Kidney dialysis is covered both at home and in an outside facility.

Some items, covered in part by Part A are covered by Part B for some of the additional costs. These include part time or intermittent **home health services** involving physical therapy, occupational therapy, speech-language pathology, as well as durable medical equipment, out-patient hospital services and supplies.

There are usually co-payments and deductibles for covered services. Ask your health care providers if they accept assignment. If they do, it means they have agreed to accept the Medicare amount as payment in full.

Services not covered

Medicare does not cover everything. Among the items not covered are acupuncture, cosmetic surgery, chiropractic care (except spine manipulation), custodial care (bathing, dressing, eating, or assisting with bathroom trips), most dental care, dentures, and some diabetic supplies (unless using an insulin pump).

Also, routine eye care, eyeglasses (except after some cataract surgery), most routine foot care, hearing aids, long term nursing home care, orthopedic shoes, routine physical exams (except once when you first enroll in Medicare), prescription drugs, shots and tests (other than those mentioned above), or most travel is not covered, although some travel may be covered in rare instances if care is available only out of the country.

Part C - Important Options to Consider

Part C is also known as Medicare Advantage Plans. These are all part of the Medicare system. They combine Part A and Part B and often offer lower premiums. There are several types:

PPO (Preferred Provider Organization):
- This plan uses doctors and hospitals within a network. Using either doctors or hospitals which are not part of the network will cost more.
- Prescription drugs are usually part of the program and the basic cost is part of the premium.
- You do not need a referral to a specialist.
- Out of network specialists may be used but usually with higher co-payments.
- You do not need to select a specific primary doctor.

HMO (Health Maintenance Organization):
- You must have a primary care physician. That doctor will act as gate-keeper for the group. If the doctor leaves, you will be notified to select another primary doctor.
- Prescription drug coverage may be part of the premium.
- You need a referral to see a specialist. In most cases, women do not need a referral for a yearly mammogram or every-other-year pelvic exam. These tests must be performed by a network doctor.
- In most cases, the specialist must be within the network. If not, you will pay higher co-payments.
- Using a doctor or facility not in the network may result in coverage being denied.
- There is also a Medicare plan which combines an HMO with Medicare. In that case, you would still pay the premiums for Part A and B and the costs would be covered if you go to a doctor outside the HMO network.

PFFS (Private Fee For Service Plan):
- You do not need to select a primary doctor.
- Drug coverage may be offered as part of the program and, if it is, will be figured in the premium.
- You can usually go to any doctor who will accept the plan's payment schedule. As long as the provider is Medicare approved (most providers in this plan are approved), there are no restrictions.
- You do not need a referral to a specialist.
- The major difference between a PFFS and original Medicare is that a PFFS is run by a private company which negotiates its own prices with providers.

Special Needs Plans:
- Designed for those with chronic diseases or other specialized health needs.
- The company must provide all the services of Part A, Part B, and Part D.
- May have other benefits and lower co-payments.
- Designed for those living in facilities like a nursing home or who need the same care as a nursing home, but are living at home.
- Patient must be eligible for both Medicare and Medicaid.
- The plan might coordinate care between doctors and other community resources, depending upon the company operating the plan.

Medical Savings Account Plans:
- Similar to a Medicare Advantage Plan, but with a higher deductible.
- Medicare may put some money in your Medical Savings Account to help defray some medical expenses.

Part D - Another "must have" program

The newest section of the Medicare program, Part D, is for prescription drug coverage. As with other parts of the program, enroll as soon as you are eligible because, if you do not, the premium will go up for every month you do not enroll. There are many companies offering this coverage. Start with the Medicare web site and follow the prompts or call 1-800-medicare if you do not have internet availability. Medicare will help you determine the actual cost of the various providers. The company you select will depend upon your medical needs. Each company has its own formulary (list of drugs covered with their lowest co-payment). Most of the companies use the same maximums but your choice of plans and pharmacy will affect how far your money will stretch.

At some point, many if not most patients will exhaust their initial coverage under Part D. At that time, the patient will be responsible for all of the costs of medication until the catastrophic level is reached. When the patient reaches the non-coverage point, there are several steps to take.

Most important, do not drop the coverage because the insurance company is no longer paying. Dropping coverage will result in a Federal Government-mandated premium penalty when you enroll again in the next year. If you are paying out-of-pocket, make sure the pharmacy continues to submit the charges to the insurance company so that coverage will begin again as soon as the patient is eligible.

If you cannot afford them, do not reduce, eliminate or substitute medications. Talk to the prescribing doctors. They may be able to substitute an equally effective substitute of lesser cost. They may also be able to provide samples of medications without cost. Ask.

You can also apply to each of the drug companies under their Patient Assistance Programs. If the patient meets the criteria, most companies will provide the medications free or at reduced cost.

You can also contact local area organizations.

If all else fails, the local welfare office may be able to assist.

If the patient exhibits serious symptoms as the result of not having medications available, the local emergency room or hospital social services department may be able to assist.

Medicare Supplement Insurance

Medicare supplements, also known as Medigap policies, are designed to fill the gaps left by the various Medicare parts. For instance, Medigap plans will pay the deductible portions of Part A and Part B. They may also pay some of the costs not covered by the original Medicare program. These plans are sold by private companies, but the government has strict controls to keep the programs consistent. The Medicare web site can help you determine who is approved to sell Medigap plans in your state.

If you have a Medigap policy which covers drugs (plan H, I, or J), and if the company sends you a letter telling you the Medigap policy is at least as good as Part D, you may keep that policy without a penalty. This does not happen very often. Generally, you should change your plan to one without drug coverage and sign up for Part D. You will get a refund or a credit from the company for the difference in premiums between the plans.

When you are ready to select a supplementary plan, you should look at the same questions you would consider when selecting any medical plan:

- Are there any extra benefits, such as dental, eye exams, out-of-country emergency care?
- Can you choose your own doctor?
- Do you need referrals for a specialist?
- Are there different charges for certain doctors? Are you limited to a particular group?
- Will the plan cover you if you spend part of the year in another state?

Check the quality ratings at the Medicare web site (www.medicare.gov or 1-800-medicare). Follow the links which begin with "Compare."

The web site will also help you by showing comparisons and giving you a list of the companies who are approved in your State. You can sign up on line.

Medicaid - When Money is a Problem

Medicaid is a welfare program, designed mostly to help low income people. The program is administered under Federal and State law. The guidelines are set by the federal government, but the program is run by each state. Within the guidelines, each state makes up its own rules. The rules allow the state to consider both income and resources. There are different rules for nursing homes, disabled children, and the elderly living at home. As a caregiver, your income will not count toward what might be covered for a child. However, there is a provision known as look-back where the State may deny or limit coverage when the patient has taken steps to reduce assets in order to qualify for benefits.

If the patient qualifies, the program will pay for most health care costs, including hospital and doctor bills, nursing home care, drug co-payments and deductibles. Depending on your income, Medicaid may also pay the Medicare premiums. You need to be sure that the doctor and facility accept Medicaid payment as payment in full. There is also a provision for reimbursement of travel expenses, based on mileage.

The best advice: When in doubt, apply. The worst case scenario is that you will not qualify. Help about programs and whether you may qualify is available at www.benefits checkup.org. Benefits Checkup is a service of the National Council for the Aging.

PACE (Program for All-Inclusive Care for the Elderly)

The goal of PACE is to help people stay independent and live in their community as long as possible, while obtaining the high quality care they need. PACE combines medical, social, and long-term care services for frail people who live and need health care in the community. This is a joint Medicare and Medicaid option in some states. To be eligible, you must be at least 55 years old, live in an area covered by the program, be eligible for nursing home care (as determined by the appropriate state agency), and be able to live safely in the community.

Other Insurance

Those in certain occupations qualify for some other programs. For instance, railroad workers have their own plan, apart from Medicare. Also, there are private plans offering a variety of coverages. We all know about life insurance and regular health insurance policies. Most private health plans expire when you are eligible for Medicare. There are also plans to guarantee a mortgage (basically a decreasing term policy), or pay for nursing home care. The limits and premiums vary so you need to research them carefully. Medicare prints a booklet which lists companies by state.

If your patient was working when he became disabled, don't forget to apply for Social Security disability insurance. This is available even if the patient is under the age of 65.

No Insurance

According to research,[11] US hospitals charge more (about 2 ½ times as much) for uninsured or out-of-pocket patients. This is the result of negotiations on the part of insurers.

The hospitals don't tell you, but another reason for having very high "regular" rates is that the government adjusts payments based upon average rates for some period of time.

If your patient has no coverage, there are several steps to take. First, remember that the hospital cannot refuse service based on ability to pay.

If your loved one has a policy with a high deductible or if the deductible has not been met, let the facility submit the bill anyway. That action should trigger the contract rate rather than the much higher self-pay rate.

Next, *negotiate*. Look for the financial assistance office or the patient accounts office. The hospital may be willing to offer a discount or help you apply for free or reduced cost care. They may also be willing to extend a discount for prompt payment.

---

[11] Originally published in Health Affairs, May/June 2007 and quoted in Today's Health & Wellness, August/September 2007.

Remember, you are not responsible for expenses incurred by your loved one. Don't pay the bill or any portion of it out of your own money. If you do, you may be legally responsible for the entire bill.

Examine the bill. Ask for an itemized invoice with all items, including "miscellaneous" entries, defined. Also, ask for the codes and their explanations. As another option, there are companies that specialize in discovering and disputing improper charges.

Finally, whenever possible, use the hospital for emergencies only. Try to wait for the doctor or use an urgent care clinic. Also, consider Hospice care (see page 100).

While this research study focused on hospitals, don't assume that only hospitals charge the uninsured at a higher rate.

Home Safety

Either you are making frequent visits to a patient or your family size has increased by one (or more). It is your responsibility as caregiver to be sure the home is safe. Check both the installation and the freshness of **batteries** for all of the safety items. These include smoke detectors, fire alarms, carbon monoxide detectors, radon detectors, and backup generators. We suggest you check the batteries twice each year and change the batteries once each year. One way to keep track is to perform the checks anytime you change the clocks (from daylight savings to standard time and back), and change the batteries on your birthday.

If the patient lives alone, instruct her not only on the operation of these **alarms**, but also on the steps to take if one goes off. The same checks and warnings are needed for the emergency life call button the patient should be wearing.

Elderly people are more susceptible to extremes of temperature. Check the aquastat on the hot water heater. Even a few degrees too hot can be dangerous for those whose reaction time to a burst of hot water can be slower than necessary.

Friends and relatives may be well-meaning and want only the best for the patient. Unfortunately, they do not always act in the best manner and usually have not been instructed on safety items.

For example, if the patient is in a **wheelchair**, the wheelchair should be locked except when moving. It does not matter whether the patient is at home or in a facility, if a well-meaning person leaves the chair unlocked, it can roll far enough to harm anyone in the area or even the patient. Many patients in wheelchairs want to lean forward or reach to pick something up. In most cases, there is no belt or other method of securing the patient. In fact, a nursing home may cite federal law provisions which dictate that the nursing home not restrain a patient without an adequate reason.[12] This action could result in a fall on the floor, where no one is around to assist the patient.

An Illustration

Yvette was in a nursing home. She made her way around the corridors in her wheelchair. When she was carrying some papers, they fell off her lap. Yvette reached for the papers and fell out of the wheelchair, receiving black and blue marks over her arms, face, hands and head. The nursing staff had to help her up. When Yvette's daughter showed up, the staff explained that she had an accident and blamed the

---

[12] Code of Federal Regulations, October 1, 2006. Title 42, Vol. 4: CITE: 42CFR483.25

resultant bruises on federal law that prevented them from belting her to the chair.

Don't always accept an explanation without investigation. Federal law does not preclude restraints when they are necessary and not just for discipline or convenience.

In other cases, the patient will rock back and forth, putting the chair at risk for tipping over. This is especially dangerous if the chair is a lightweight model. A heavier chair may be harder to move around but the lower center of gravity makes it harder for it to tip over.

Well-meaning people often try to help a patient, either getting out of the chair or pushing the chair to another location. Some of these friends may have their own medical problems, involving the heart, back, or discs. They may even be recovering from surgery but want to be helpful. While it is good that some-one wants to help, good intentions may result in your having another patient in need of care.

When your patient is in a wheelchair, be sure both wheels are locked before trying to help the patient stand up. When talking to a person in a wheelchair, get down to her level. Keep the chair adjusted so the patient can keep her feet on the foot plates. Don't let her retract the plates. Move the patient occasionally to avoid bed sores. Warn her if you are about to move the chair or have her stand up.

The presence of a patient can make the home like an obstacle course. **Long telephone cords and extra long oxygen tubing** make it easier for a patient to get around the home, but also can cause falls by the patient or a visitor. Visitors and family members must also take care not to step on the oxygen tube, thereby cutting off the oxygen supply. Grab bars, installed in the bathroom, may come out of the wall when a patient is holding on, if not instal-led properly. Supervision is always necessary.

Many patients are on **blood thinning drugs**. There is a greater risk in the event of a fall or a cut. Shaving should be done with an electric razor, rather than a blade. Make certain that the wood on chairs, tables or other furnishings does not have splinters and that the screws and other fasteners are secure.

Family members get used to a **bed** and its height almost as a matter of course. A patient, however, may not be so lucky. A bed which is too high may cause a fall. A patient may have trouble getting into or out of a bed which is either too high or too low. If the bed is electric, check the mechanism for wear and tear and for proper operation. Regularly check the mattress for wear and tear and for deep depressions, which may be sign of a defect.

Choosing **clothes** is easy for most family members. A patient, however, may have trouble. You should put lights in the closet and make sure the items are hanging at a height the patient can reach easily. The clothes may also be a problem. Some patients have difficulty with small buttons or zippers. Clothes can be adapted to make dressing easier. If a patient has difficulty tying shoelaces, for example, shoes are available with Velcro closings. There are many catalogs available which show these helpful items. Talk to the patient's therapists for some more guidance in this area. These needs may not always be identified in the doctor's office because the setting is different.

You may need to place some **vision or hearing** devices in the home, for example, to make it easier to enlarge the type in newspapers, or to hear the television without the volume at its highest setting. Do not be afraid to ask as many people as needed.

One way to minimize germs and therefore illness is frequent hand washing. As with anything else, there is a right way and a wrong way. Don't scrub. Scrubbing can cause cracks in the skin which will harbor bacteria. Rather, wash well, take your time, and be thorough. Proper hand washing should take at least 15 seconds. That is about the time it takes to sing *Mary Had a Little Lamb*. If you don't know the words, try the *Happy Birthday* song. Equally important is thorough drying. Wet hands are more likely than dry hands to spread germs. If you use hand sanitizers, which are alcohol based, be sure to cover all parts of your hands and wrists. Since these products don't need to be dried, using a bit too much is better than not using enough.

Protect Against Falls

Falls are the seventh leading cause of death in persons over the age of 65.[13] Falls in and around the home can have serious consequences. The good news is there are many steps that can minimize the problem.

Many factors contribute to the increase in accidents. Normal aging plays a role but we can't control that. Poor eyesight, poor hearing, more frequent illnesses, deteriorating physical condition, poor reflexes, and medication side effects are some of the causes beyond our control.

By the year 2040, it is expected that about 750,000 hip fractures will put about 150,000 patients in long term nursing care.[14]

There are, however, causes we can control. These are environmental; surroundings, light-

---

[13] Originally reported in the New England Journal of Medicine and quoted in: "25 ways to Protect Yourself (Or Someone You Care For) From Falls," Philips Lifeline website (www.lifelinesys.com).
[14] Chartbook on Women and Disability in the United States, National Institute on Disability and Rehabilitation Research, US Department of Education, 1999.

ing, and other items that need attention. Those are the things to focus on as a caregiver.

Some of these items may have been mentioned earlier but there is no substitute for safety. While we are quick to cure, prevention is easier and cheaper. In and around the house:

- Wear shoes with non-skid soles (not slippers) - both patient and caregiver
- Do not walk in stockings or socks
- Make sure the home is well lit
- Keep light switches within easy reach
- Have lights at the top and bottom of staircases
- Keep stairs in good repair with no loose or uneven steps
- Turn on the lights when entering at night
- Pad or remove sharp edges on appliances and countertops
- Keep counter space near the stove clear
- Use night lights (bedroom, bathroom, hallways, and stairways)
- Keep a flashlight handy
- Have a telephone within easy reach (cordless is preferable)
- Keep emergency numbers in large print near every phone
- Remove throw rugs (or tape the ends down)
- Keep furniture where no one will trip over it
- Make sure rugs and other flooring are flat
- When possible, use low pile carpeting
- Remove cords from pathways
- Have a professional put grab bars in the bathtub shower, and toilet area
- Use mats with suction cups or non-skid strips in the shower or tub
- Use a bench in the shower

- Set the water temperature to 120 degrees or below
- Consider an elevated toilet seat
- Have handrails on both sides of stairways
- Have light switches on both ends of stairways
- Have lights on both sides of the bed
- Make sure stair rugs are firmly attached and are not slippery or worn
- Keep floors free of clutter
- Don't allow patients to climb on stools and stepladders (Get help)
- Never allow patients to stand on a chair to reach
- Keep frequently used items in drawers and cabinets within easy reach
- Make sure floor surfaces are clean and dry
- Use non-skid wax (or don't wax at all)
- Sidewalks and walkways need to be kept in good repair
- Remove snow and ice from sidewalks and walkways
- Keep stairs and walkways free of clutter
- Use sand liberally
- Check surfaces - temperatures change as do walking conditions
- Paint outdoor stairs with non-slip paint or mix sand in the paint

There are also medical steps and instructions you need to take and reinforce. Sometimes, patients don't like to do what they should. You need to watch for signs of resistance.

An Illustration

Honora lived alone, but had a heart condition. Her son, who lived two hours away told her to tell the ambulance driver to take her to a nearby heart institute if she had a problem. When Honora experienced chest discomfort, she dialed 9-1-1 but had the paramedics take her to her local hospital. When her son asked why she did not go to the heart institute, Honora replied, "I didn't want to bother anyone."

When the elderly insist on living alone, especially far from family, impress upon them the need to go to the best facility, not always the most convenient, unless it is an immediate life-threatening emergency.

Eye tests should be conducted every year, especially in the elderly. Cataracts, glaucoma and other eye problems tend to appear more often as the patient ages.

Hearing should be checked at least every two years. Pay special attention if you think there are any changes in hearing behavior, such as the television being turned louder and louder.

Foot pain should result in a doctor consultation. Corns should be attended to professionally. If you can trim the patient's toenails, that is all right. If not, you should let the podiatrist do it, even though that charge is not covered by insurance.

Consult the doctor immediately if a **medication** is making the patient lose his balance or feel dizzy. Even if not caused by medications, feelings of weakness, light-headedness or dizziness should be addressed as soon as possible.

An Illustration

Isaac had a stroke. After a stay in a nursing home, he was sent for rehabilitation. In the rehabilitation center, the physical therapist gave him a walker and told him to use it at all times. Isaac resisted, told his wife he refused to use the walker, and threw it against the wall. On his next regular checkup, Isaac walked unsteadily into the doctor's office -- without the walker. The doctor was upset and told Isaac that if he did not use the walker, he would be sent back to the nursing home.

Be firm. If the patient requires a walker, make sure it is used. Do not hesitate to keep the therapist involved in this issue.

Canes and walkers need to be fitted for the patient. Do not obtain either of these items without having them properly fitted. Make sure the patient uses them. A cane or walker sitting in the corner will last a long time, but will serve no purpose.

If the patient requires frequent trips to the **bathroom** but cannot walk or get around well, consider a bedside commode, especially if the trips are in the middle of the night.

When the patient gets up, either in the middle of the night or in the morning, require her to sit on the side of the bed for a minute or two before standing. That will allow blood pressure to adjust and will reduce dizziness and falls.

Exercise is most effective when done regularly. Walking is especially valuable. There is no reason to speed. The act itself is good for patients and promotes health. For those suffering from arthritis, exercise is especially valuable, even when the joints are aching. Talk first with the doctor to determine which exercise activities are appropriate. A well-rounded exercise program will include stretching for flexibility, resistance to build strength, and aerobics that improve heart and lungs.

Important in any exercise plan is appropriate preparation. Always warm up before exercise and cool down afterward. Warm up and cool down can be as simple as stretching.

Wait at least two hours after eating. Consult the doctor after a cold.

Slow down when going uphill. Even a slight incline adds to the amount of work.

Dress in loose, comfortable clothes, appropriate to the weather. Pay particular attention to the shoes. Although a good pair of shoes should last up to 500 miles, it is often difficult to tell when they no longer provide the support they should. Many people may not realize when their shoes are wearing out or no longer supply appropriate support.

Plan for the weather. Watch for overheating in hot or humid weather. If the heat or humidity is oppressive, exercise early in the day or in the early evening.

Drink plenty of water. It is important to remain hydrated.

Discuss the patient's exercise program with her doctor. Together, you can determine appropriate limitations.

Stop exercising if the patient:
- Feels discomfort, like aching, burning, fullness or tightness
- Begins wheezing (if that is not normal for the patient)
- Experiences shortness of breath (if not normal)
- Feels pain in the bones or joints (if not normal)
- Can't finish the exercise session
- Can't carry on a conversation while exercising (if not normal)
- Feels faint (if not normal)
- Feels fatigue (if not normal)
- Had difficulty sleeping after exercise.

Don't be afraid to visit the doctor if any of these symptoms persist or if you are concerned.

Alcohol is allowed for most people. As with most things, moderation is the key. Two drinks or less a day is generally considered safe. More than that can cause unsteadiness. You also need to check medications for an alcohol ban. Some medications can lose their potency if the patient uses alcohol. Also, some patients can't tolerate alcohol and should abstain from its use altogether.

There is no such thing as moderation for **smoking**. Not only should the patient not smoke, neither should the caregiver or visitors to the house. Second hand smoke can be just as harmful as smoking. Further, if a lit cigarette is left unattended, fire can occur. The danger is multiplied if anyone is using oxygen in the household.

Safety and Security

Some safety items are either ignored or bypassed in many families. Ignoring these items can be dangerous when the household includes an elderly or disabled person. Avoid fire hazards:

- Check all electrical outlets and be sure they are not overloaded
- Be sure that all circuits are GFI-protected to reduce the chance of shocks
- Remove all hazardous and flammable materials
- Use extension cords properly (don't attach an extension cord to another extension cord)
- Don't use larger wattage light bulbs than the fixtures can handle
- Check the batteries often on all smoke detectors (a good rule of thumb is to check the detectors when you change the clocks forward or back and change the batteries on your birthday)
- Never use a larger capacity circuit breaker than appropriate

- Be careful if and when you use space heaters
- Teach everyone how to report a fire (preprogram 9-1-1 into every telephone)

In addition to keeping your home safe and minimize the chance of a deadly fire, you need to keep the home secure.

- Make sure all doors and windows have locks and that those locks are all working properly
- Doors should have peep holes
- Do not open the door to strangers
- Check identification before allowing entry
  - Call the utility company to verify that a service technician is in the area
  - Call the local police station to verify the identity of a police officer or that a salesperson is properly licensed
- Keep all outside areas well-lit
- Trim bushes and plants so the view is not obstructed
- Keep a phone handy
  - A cell phone is preferable
- Keep emergency numbers at every phone

Transportation

Many cities have low cost rides available for the elderly or disabled. Some offer rides to the local senior center or to restaurants, activities and other events. Some hospitals even have vans that offer pick up and delivery service for medical appointments. Organizations and churches often have volunteers who will drive a patient to and from medical appointments or other events. Look also for discount passes.

Often, a patient wants to keep his driver's license. He will insist that he is still capable of driving. You need to determine whether that is true or not.

An Illustration

George renewed his driving license, including the parallel parking portion. He received his license in the mail about a week later. He limited his driving to the local grocery store, gas station and the senior center. George drives only about 7,500 miles each year and claimed to have owned 10 to 15 cars in his lifetime, beginning with a Model T Ford. Sometimes, his 64 year old son follows to "make sure he's doing okay." George was renewing his license because he just celebrated his birthday... His 101st.[15]

Age is important to consider, but, alone, is not a reason to deny someone a license.

If you are going to provide transportation, use a **handicap decal**, placard or plate. They can be issued when a medical disability makes it hard for the patient get around. A physician can write a letter and fill out a special form which needs to be submitted to the Registry of Motor Vehicles.

Some conditions are easy to see: for instance, a patient may be in a wheelchair. Other conditions are hidden, such as the use of a pacemaker, heart condition, or lung disorder.

In some cases, the disability is permanent. Other times, the condition might be temporary, like a broken leg.

The important thing is that the patient must have difficulty walking a distance or walking at all. When using a handicap placard, sticker or plate, parking is allowed in spaces

---

[15] This UPI story was originally reported in the (Everett, WA) Daily Herald and adapted from the Weird News Newsletter, © 2007 by ArcaMax Publishing, Inc.

near the door of a physician's office, hospital, or supermarket. A certain number of spaces are required by law and must be clearly labeled. If you park at a parking meter, no fee is required.

The only restriction is that the patient must be in the car. Do not use the disability plate when the patient is not in the car.

When the application form is completed and sent to the motor vehicle department, it should be processed in a timely manner. It should not take months. If there is a chance that the patient's health or safety could be harmed by a long wait, ask for a supervisor and explain the problem. If the request is denied, there are appeals available. Check with the doctor and with the motor vehicle department in your state.

If you are doing the driving, don't neglect the tax allowance on your income tax returns. The IRS allows for an allowance which can be either a per-mile or actual cost computation.

Take the bus

When a facility is not nearby, consider taking public transportation. Conditions, such as the weather, may influence your ability to drive a distance. A patient may not be able to sit through a long ride in your car but may be able to make the trip by train or bus.

Parking must be considered as part of the overall transportation cost. Many garages and parking lots are expensive. If you must drive to a hospital, ask the hospital social services department about discounts.

If a bus is used for a long trip and the patient is on oxygen, see the tips in the next section. All oxygen must be stored in a well ventilated area.

Long Distance Travel

If you are planning to travel a distance, especially by airplane, you need to plan ahead.

First, check with your patient's doctor to be sure that the trip being planned will not have any adverse effects. All travel, especially by air, has stress, and your patient and you need to be able to handle it. If your plans involve a variety of altitudes, prescription doses may need to be adjusted.

Next, ask the doctor for a copy of all prescriptions, in case refills are needed during the trip. Keep those prescriptions where you can find them, and not in luggage you can't get to or which can be lost.

Check with your insurance company to be sure that anything needed will be covered.

If the patient is on oxygen, there are other considerations. Most airlines have very strict regulations. Because of Federal Aviation Administration rules, the only on-board oxygen which is allowed must be provided by the airline (very expensive) and must be ordered well in advance. Some allow oxygen concentrators as a carry on, but only if it does not require airplane power. Ask the airline, including connecting flight carriers, and your oxygen supplier. For a list of some suppliers, see Appendix G (page 197).

Most suppliers can arrange to have oxygen delivered to your destination, including intermediate destinations on a long trip.

If you need to refill a portable device, make sure the procedure is completed in a well-ventilated area.

Don't store oxygen in the trunk of a car or in the baggage area of a plane, bus, or train.

Amtrak allows oxygen, subject to some requirements. As with all travel arrangements, consult with the company well ahead of time.

If the patient will need assistance at an airport or intermediate bus depot, check with each airport or location through which you will travel.

If the patient will be traveling alone, most airlines can provide a higher level of assistance. As with other arrangements, ask the airline as well as all connecting carriers.

The questions which must be answered include information on cost, available equipment, capacity, and assistance. Some of the airline requirements are listed in Appendix F (page 188).

Newspapers, Magazines and Publications

Most states and the Federal government offer free booklets and information that is useful for caregivers. They can be sent to your home. If you have computer access, start with www.gpoaccess.gov. Your local library can also help find the booklets and brochures you want. Among other things, you can find answers to most simple legal issues and details on accommodations and other assistance for which your patient may be eligible.

Many newspapers offer discount rates for seniors and disabled people. You simply need to ask.

Sleep

Do not underestimate the need for sleep. According to one article,[16] causes of sleep deprivation are related to lifestyle, health complications, medication side effects, and clinical disorders.

Call the doctor when:
- The patient snores excessively

---

[16] Morefocus Group Inc. © 2007, http://sleep deprivation.com

- The patient uses sleeping pills excessively
- The patient suffers from nightmares
- The patient chokes
- The patient appears to stop breathing
- The patient suffers from insomnia most nights in a month
- Tiredness affects daily activities on a regular basis (more than normally)
- Symptoms include shortness of breath, chest pain, or other alarming conditions

Lifestyle choices which may affect sleeping include drinking caffeine or alcohol close to bedtime.

Many medications have side effects which include sleep problems.

Medical conditions, such as asthma and mental health problems, may make sleep difficult. Mental health issues may involve depression and post-traumatic stress disorder.

If there is an underlying disorder, the treatment of that disorder may improve sleep.

Different people require different amounts of sleep. Some may get by with as little as 3-4 hours of sleep. The norm is closer to 6-9 hours per night.

Sleeping Arrangements

Elderly people and people with handicaps require modifications which you may not even think to consider. A patient may require night lights, a flashlight, soft bedding, proximity to the bathroom, even rails or similar supports. The floors should not be slippery. Scatter rugs may serve only to scatter the patient. Also necessary are safe and easy-to-use shades and curtains, proper heating and cooling mechanisms. Patients, especially the elderly, have heating requirements different from everyone else. Many are always cold, so supply extra blankets and sweaters.

There should also be nearby call buttons, intercoms, fluids, chairs that allow one to get up easily, furniture with corners that do not jut out. It is also helpful that any door locking or closing mechanism give a warning when entering the room to avoid any possible physical harm to those who enter or use the room.

Be sure that headboards and footboards are secure and checked for wear and splinters. Alarm systems should be operational and checked. Have a backup plan for cooling and heating in the event of a power failure. A clear path for walking is required. A cordless telephone is better than one with a long cord.

Support Groups

Many hospitals, clinics and colleges offer classes and group meetings for support. Ask the hospital elders program or social service office for a list. You can also find groups through the local newspapers. There are usually programs about nutrition, diabetes management, driving, exercise, or tax preparation, to name some. These programs may be free or involve a small fee.

You can also start your own support group. The hospital coffee shop is a good way to meet other people with similar needs. If you are in a group, there are many guest speakers available. They will be happy to meet with your group for free and are available for a wide variety of subjects. Discuss this possibility with the various state and hospital elder services departments.

There is nothing as valuable as knowledge to help you be the best caregiver possible.

Respite

In addition to support groups, there are other sources you can take advantage of.

To get time away to recharge your 'batteries,' consider local programs offering adult day care. These programs provide social interaction for patients as well as providing rest for you. In some cases, transportation is also available.

Other home care services, like the Visiting Nurses Association in your area, can provide help at home by nurses or home-health aides. They can help in many areas, including help with bathing, dressing, eating, and even housekeeping.

There are also for-pay services which offer a form of respite care including pets, housekeeping, senior care, and even babysitting. One such company is Care.com (www.care.com). An internet search may find others.

Hospice agencies work with terminally ill patients who live at home. They offer an opportunity for the caregiver to enjoy some relief, become education and gain support.

There are also programs which provide regular phone calls to check on the well being of elderly patients, especially those living on their own.

The US Administration on Aging, part of the Department of Health and Human Services, offers an eldercare locator. The resources are available at www.eldercare.com or by calling 1-888-3897-8839, weekdays from 9:00 a.m. to 8:00 p.m. eastern time. Spanish language assistance is also available.

Self Care

Support groups may offer you help and comfort. In addition to the help offered by those groups, there are other steps to make your job easier.

Share decisions and decision making with the patient if possible. When she is part of the decision, she will be more apt to accept the decision.

Get help from other family members. As with your patient, family members will be more open and more accepting of your decisions. Their assistance will also make your life a bit easier. You will also benefit from their emotional support.

Family assistance will also allow you the respite care you will need to retain your own mental health. It is imperative that you get away occasionally to relax, either alone or with your own family.

Take the time to do the research. Having all the information about the patent's condition or illness makes it easier to cope with setbacks or with the normal course of the condition. The research will also allow for proper future planning.

Money Concerns

Most patients, especially those with chronic conditions, worry about finances. They are concerned about paying for costs beyond their insurance, or they do not have insurance at all. There are steps you can take to reduce the stress.

Apply for everything you need. The worst thing that can happen is a denial. When you get a denial for any service, file an appeal if there is any chance at all that the decision can be reversed. Among those you need to contact are Social Security, Medicare, Medicaid, local welfare departments, hospitals and drug companies.

Most of the drug companies today offer free or low-cost prescription service for those unable to afford their drugs. Every manufacturer is different and each has a different application. Ask your doctor for help in applying. Do not hesitate to ask your doctor for samples. Most drug companies provide doctors with samples to use as the doctor sees fit.

Ask the hospital social service department for their help. They can assist you in applying for various programs. Local welfare departments also offer emergency assistance for items which can range from food to prescriptions.

If the patient needs a hospital for any reason, don't hesitate to go there. Do not worry about insurance coverage. All hospitals are required to offer care regardless of a person's ability to pay.

Take advantage of free screenings which are scheduled periodically at clinics or even at the local mall.

There is even low- or no-cost legal service available when needed.

Among the items for which help is available is the preparation of the various documents mentioned earlier (see page 20). Trained volunteers and volunteer professionals are available to help prepare such items as a durable power of attorney, or a living will and to provide assistance with financial planning, taxes, social security and disability benefits, as well as other public benefits.

While doing all these tasks, reassure the patient that she will still get the care needed.

Assistance

Everyone knows about calling 9-1-1 for emergencies and 4-1-1 for information. In many parts of the country, there is another option. More than one-half of the population can now dial 2-1-1 to be connected to a professional who can help determine your particular need and put you in contact with the appropriate agency.

In at least some areas, assistance is available on topics which include domestic violence, gambling addiction, financial problems, suicide prevention, and substance abuse.

Staff members can help with everything from counseling for a teen who won't go to school to transportation for a patient who is disabled.

When you are not sure where to find help, this may be a good place to start.

Time Off From Work

When you need to, the law allows you to take time off from work to care for an immediate family member. This law, know as the **Family and Medical Leave Act (FMLA)** covers you if you have been employed with the same company for at least 12 months and for at least 24 hours per week. The company must have at least 50 employees. You may take a total of 12 weeks of *unpaid* leave per year for any of the following reasons:

- The birth and care of your newborn child
- To adopt or accept a child be becoming a foster parent
- To care for an immediate family member with a serious health condition[17]
- To take a medical leave when you are unable to work because of **your** serious health condition

The rules are different for those who work for any government agency, serve in the armed forces or in an approved school. Parts of the law are outlined in Appendix D (page 167).

The rules listed here and in Appendix D are Federal minimums. States, cities, individual companies, union contracts, or individual contracts may provide a wider range of coverage.

---

[17] An immediate family member is defined as a spouse, child, or parent.

Medical Concerns

Now that your patient is comfortable and your house is ready, you need to be prepared to face the issues of care. Lay people do not always have the time, resources, support or the ability to assess medical and psychological care of their loved one, especially when important decisions need to be made. Caregivers agonize over both small and large issues. Information makes a big difference. Reduce your stress level by seeking a second or even a third opinion. You should not make every decision alone. Sometimes, a patient needs a different doctor, or even a different facility. At other times, you may need to file a complaint to get the service or level of care the patient needs. Issues can even rise to the level of requiring legal assistance, financial assistance, or debt consolidation.

One place which is of concern is the hospital. While people go to the hospital to get cured, it is also a place to get sick. Government studies show that, each year, 1.7 million Americans get infections in the hospital and 99,000 of them die. To make sure your patient does not leave the hospital sicker than when she arrived, insist upon proper cleanliness. In many cases, professionals wash their hands after seeing a patient. They then handle doorknobs, charts, and phones, all of which are germ laden. Ask your doctor, therapist, or even your visitors to wash their hands.

There are many places to turn when you are having a problem with an issue. Some of them include:

- National or local organizations that specialize in the specific disorder affecting the patient
- The Ombudsman for your state (Not every state has one)
- Advocates from the state

- The citizen referral line or help line from the state
- State approved mental health centers or agencies in the city
- Lawyer referral center or legal assistance agency for disabled people
- Local hospital support groups or referral lines
- Condition-specific support groups
- Senior citizen councils or agencies in your town
- The city listing in the phone book
  o Look for local services. Most are listed in the phone book under "[your city], town of."
- Transportation programs for the elderly and handicapped
- Medical supply stores
- Licensed social workers
- Psychologists who specialize in the patient's illness
- Pharmacists
- Meals on Wheels
- Members of the Clergy

Do not let a lack of funds stop you from obtaining information, referrals or help. Even the lack of insurance should not prevent you from getting help.

Another stress reducer is laughter. The Mayo Foundation has reported that a chuckle can stimulate the heart, lungs and muscles, help digestion and circulation, and relieve pain.

Insure Quality

Even when the patient is living with you (or alone), there will be times when you and the patient will interact with doctors, nurses, therapists, hospitals and other professionals. During these times, you may question whether the care is appropriate. There are signs to watch for.

First, the professional should never be too busy to explain what is happening, including information on any medications the patient is using. Ask what the medication is, what it is meant to help, whether it is the best or most economical drug for the patient, and if the drug will have any side effects or if it will react with any other medications the patient is taking. Also, ask how long it will be before the drug takes effect.

If your medication makes the news, don't be afraid to ask if your dose is still appropriate or if there is an alternative. In many cases, despite dire news in the media, the medication may still be the best choice for the patient. It is possible that not taking the medication is worse than the side effects of the medication. In any event, having the discussion may be the catalyst which causes the doctor to consider other options. Don't stop taking medications, even non-prescription items, such as vitamins or aspirin, until you speak with the doctor. Often, the benefits will far outweigh the possible risks.

Make sure medications are appropriate for the condition and not a drug with a similar name. Make sure the drug has not been the subject of a recall. If the patient is elderly, make sure the drug is not one which should never be taken by elderly patients.

You should have a list of all medications and their doses with you. In many cases, a patient has more than one doctor, each working within a different specialty. Each needs to be aware of any medications which have been prescribed by other professionals.

If a therapist is working in a specific area, for example walking skills, you should be told what is being done and why. You should also know what the expected results will be and how long it will take to see any progress. At the same time, don't be alarmed or upset if the therapist answers that she doesn't know. "I don't know," is acceptable in many cases, at least for a while.

An Illustration

Javier suffered from heart disease. He was 82 years old. After he complained about stomach symptoms a doctor examined him and performed some tests. He then indicated that Javier had developed cancer. The doctor suggested that an operation was needed. His daughter asked about the operation, including its success rate, the likelihood that Javier would survive the operation and how long it would take to progress. The doctor indicated that the cancer would be fatal in the next 5-10 years. Javier's daughter refused to allow the operation.

No action is sometimes the best course of action.

If a doctor indicates that an operation is needed, you need all the details of the operation before you give consent.

A specialist usually works within his specialty. Sometimes, little thought is given to things not within that specialty. An operation may have marginal benefit but at the cost of loss of quality life in the meantime. Some people believe that one good year is better than 15 months of existence. You should know what the patient wants and make the best, most informed decision you can.

Ask Questions

Prepare ahead of time. Bring a written list of questions every time you visit the doctor, hospital or specialist. Get answers to every question on your list and do not leave before every one of them is answered and that you understand the answer. If the answer is in medical terms you don't understand, persist and ask for clarification until you are satisfied.

Screening Tests

There are tests available to screen for virtually everything. The question to discuss with the doctor is whether a particular test is appropriate or beneficial for the patient. That discussion should also consider whether a particular test will be covered by insurance.

Balance

Falls are the leading cause of injury deaths among older people. About nine percent of adults 65 and older report balance problems. Moreover, according to the Centers for Disease Control and Prevention, more than one-third of those 65 and older fall each year.[18] Add to that the number of people who do not report the problem or who pretend the problem does not exist. Good balance means being able to control and maintain body position. The patient should be able to walk without staggering, get up from a chair without falling and climb stairs without tripping. The main cause of balance problems is a disturbance of the inner ear.

Regular exercise is one way to reduce the chances for a fall. If your patient is allowed to by her doctor, there are many forms of exercise available.

A yearly eye exam may discover glaucoma or cataracts or the wrong glasses. An inability to see properly can increase the chance of falling.

[18] National Institutes of Health, Senior Health, Balance Problems, last reviewed January, 2007.

Keep the home as fall-proof as possible, with grab bars, non-skid floors, non-slip rugs, and a minimum of things which can cause tripping.

A patient may not admit to having a balance problem and may insist that nothing is wrong. The symptoms of balance problems include a feeling of lightheadedness; fainting; blurred vision; disorientation; losing the sense of time, place, or identity; or falling. The patient will feel unsteady or as if she is moving, floating, or spinning (vertigo).

If you think the patient has a balance disorder, schedule an appointment with the doctor. To help with a diagnosis, write down everything you can about what happened, when and how. Include any suspicions, even if the patient insists that "it was nothing." The doctor will want a description of the balance or dizziness problem, how often it occurs, and whether the patient has fallen down and, if so, how often, where and when.

As in all cases, the doctor will want a complete list of medications, including over-the-counter remedies which could impact balance.

Medications

The biggest problem with medications occurs when they are not taken or when only some of them are taken. According to the American Society of Health-System Pharmacists, more than half of all Americans take more than one medication daily. Skipped pills rarely work as designed. Nor are medications as effective as they should be when doses are skipped, stopped before the doctor said they should be, or not taken at all. According to research, two-thirds of all medications are not taken either occasionally or at all. Only one-sixth of people follow the prescriptions as ordered.[19]

There are many techniques to help make certain the patient takes his medications correctly. Ideas range from a simple chart to more involved gadgets.

A **chart**, which can be kept on the refrigerator door, should contain the drug, dose or strength, doctor, why it was prescribed, when it should be taken (such as, breakfast, dinner, 4 p.m.), the date it started, and if appropriate, the last day it should be taken. Include on that list, both prescription medications and over-the-counter remedies. Do not fail to include everything, down to daily vitamins. Many medications must be taken until the bottle is finished. If the patient does not finish the medications, even when "feeling better," a relapse of the condition is possible. We have included a chart for your use (see appendix H, beginning on page 201).

If a chart is not enough, companies sell a pillbox, a container with compartments which designate days or even the time of day. Some of these may be available for free from some of the drug companies. They are given as promotional items.

A **timer** will help some people. Options are a programmable watch, a beeper of some sort, or even an alarm clock.

If you feel more comfortable with your cell phone or other wireless communication device, there are companies which let you create and send yourself personalized reminders. Two are www.caretext.com and www.OnTimeRx.com.

Other options do not involve outside companies. You should know what each medication is for. Write that information on the

---

[19] Why Should You Take Your Medications? How Can You Remember To? © Harvard Health Publications. May, 2007. Distributed by Gather.com.

bottle. Know how it should be taken (such as, with food, on an empty stomach, an hour before eating).

Out of sight is out of mind. Keep the patient's pills where you can see them (unless there are young children present who could get into them). For instance, on the kitchen table or even next to your toothbrush may help. Count out the day's dosage at the same time every day. Some caregivers may find it helpful to put them out the night before. Others may find it useful to put morning pills near the coffee pot and evening pills near the hand lotion you use every night.

Make medications part of the day. Always take them at the same time. Make associations between a pill and some task, like walking the dog or eating lunch.

When all else fails, enlist family and friends. Nothing can work better than a support system.

As with all medications, you need to monitor the patient's progress. The medicine should do what it was designed to do. Any side effect should be reported to the doctor immediately. In some cases, the side effects cannot be avoided, while in other cases, a different drug might be prescribed.

Continue all medications even if you don't see immediate results. Some medications are preventative while others may take time to reverse a condition which may have taken a long time to develop.

If the medication is not taken regularly, that is, it is prescribed to be taken "as needed," ask your pharmacist what the real expiration date is. By law, the pharmacy will put an expiration date on the bottle which is, at most, one year after the prescription was filled. But the larger container the pharmacist has will have a different, later date. Insist that the pharmacist tells you that date, even when they don't want to. Write that date on the bottle. Drugs start to lose their effectiveness after they have expired. You should throw them away after the expiration date.

There are other tips to think about. Keep all medications in their original container. Follow the instructions about storing them. Some may require refrigeration, others not. Some pills are meant to be taken whole. Ask the pharmacist before crushing them or cutting them in half. In some cases, not taking them whole is a problem. In other cases, cutting a pill in half may result in a cost saving because the higher dose pill may be less expensive overall. Review your medication list with the doctor at least once each year - more often if you change prescriptions regularly.

Another important part of taking medications is understanding the instructions.

An Illustration

Wanda took her toddler son to the pediatrician when he complained of an earache. Since this was Wanda's first child, she listened carefully to the doctor's instructions. She was told to use the medications three times each day for ten days. Wanda diluted the medication in water and made the child drink the mixture, carefully recording the times each day when the medications were administered. After ten days, the toddler continued to scream in pain. Wanda returned to the doctor, who asked if she was careful to put the medications in the right ear.

You need to understand the instructions clearly and completely.

Save Money on Medications

When you spend so much money on medications that you don't want to think about it, is exactly the time when you should think about it. There are steps you should take before not taking a medication becomes the patient's action of choice.

Ask the doctor to help. Normally, doctors don't think of cost when selecting a medication to prescribe. When you mention the difficulty of paying, however, the doctor will generally pay more attention to the problem. Most people can take generic versions of drugs. Generics have been approved by the Food and Drug Administration and are the same as the brand name, but at much lower cost. Another option is for the doctor to select a less expensive alternative which will accomplish the same purpose. You can also ask for a prescription which will cover a longer period of time. In many cases, an insurance company will save you money on co-payments when you order a larger quantity. If the drugs are equivalent, ask for a higher dosage pill and cut them in half. This may be significantly less expensive. Do not get a higher dosage if the pills cannot be cut in half and retain their effectiveness.

Conversely, sometimes a smaller dose can work.

An Illustration

Xavier had a prescription for 150 mg tablets of a medication. The doctor indicated that this would be a maintenance dose which Xavier would take for an extended period. Xavier's insurance plan had a coverage limit which he reached every year. His pharmacist suggested that Xavier purchase a lower dose of the same medication, available over the counter, and take two tablets. The cost to Xavier for two tablets at the lower dose was less than his out-of-pocket cost for a single tablet of the higher dose.

The pharmacist can be a valuable resource and can save you money if your doctor agrees that the total dose is equivalent.

Shop around. Not every pharmacy is created equal. Some drug stores are less expensive than others, but that may vary, depending upon the specific drugs the patient is taking.

An Illustration

Loretta heard many advertisements on television and in magazines about mail order pharmacies which would give her three months worth of drugs for two co-payments. Loretta was on Medicare and required multiple prescriptions. Medicare plans record the amount spent by the insurance company as well as the amount spent by the patient. The total of those charges is the amount which has a limit. After the limit is reached, the patient is required to pay the entire amount of the medications for the next $2,000. Loretta decided to discuss the situation with her pharmacist. Because the pharmacy charged less for her drugs overall, Loretta found that she could get through the entire year without reaching the limit, but with the mail order service, she would be paying the entire bill for the last several months of the year.

When comparing options, consider the total cost for the year, not the immediate cost for a specific drug alone.

When you shop competitively, work on the *entire* list. While you can certainly buy one medication at one shop and another elsewhere, you will lose the advantage of having one pharmacist or drug store familiar with all of the patient's needs, a situation which will allow for the constant checking for drugs which should not be taken together or for drugs which cross-react with other medications, allergies or conditions. You can also shop online. Today, most drug stores have on-line sites which may offer discounts over their storefront outlets. One step you can take is to see if the site has a seal of approval from the National Association of Boards of Pharmacy. To check a specific pharmacy, go to www.nabp.net and click on Accreditation Programs. Select VIPPS (Verified Internet Pharmacy Practice Sites).

When you receive a medication from the pharmacy, look at it. You should recognize if the pills look different. If you are not sure, ask the pharmacist. Generic drugs from different manufacturers may not look the same even though the active ingredients are identical. A pharmacy will dispense whichever brand they purchased at the best price. The manufacturer may change frequently. Don't be embarrassed if you need to ask if the medication is identical in active ingredients and in dose.

You can also join a group. Some organizations, such as AARP, offer plans for little cost which gain a discount on many widely used drugs. As with other steps, check to be sure the savings will be real and not just savings off "the retail price."

Some drug companies offer their own discount program for more than 150 of the more popularly prescribed medications. Most drug companies also have programs to supply drugs for free to those who cannot afford them. Ask your doctor for information and assistance.

Surgery

In the event that a test or surgery is indicated, you should ask when and where you will get the results. Do not accept the answer that the doctor will call only if there is a problem. That answer may be acceptable for a young, otherwise healthy person, but is not one to accept for a patient who requires a caregiver.

Equally important to getting the results is learning where the test or procedure will be performed. Talk to the doctor about which facility offers the best care for the type of service the patient needs. A hospital known for great heart care may not be the best facility for diabetes. You should also consider whether the facility is close enough for you to be there when the procedure is performed. In smaller cities and towns, most of the doctors maintain an affiliation at more than one facility. If not, the doctor will try to steer you toward the facility with which he is affiliated. Do not be afraid to select a different facility if you feel more comfortable with that choice. Start with Medline Plus or one of the other rating sites. On occasion, this step might mean you need to change doctors, at least for the procedure in question.

If the procedure involves a test which may lead to surgery, make your decisions with the surgery in mind. Then, if surgery is required, make sure to share the information on medications and allergies with the surgeon, anesthesiologist and the nurses. You cannot repeat this information too many times.

Before all surgery, be sure the patient complies with all the instructions. Pay attention to orders for everything from antibiotics to pre-confinement cleaning. All pills should be taken on schedule and completely except for aspirin and products containing aspirin. Ask the doctor how far in advance aspirin should be discontinued. If an anti-bacterial soap is prescribed, follow the instructions carefully.

When surgery is indicated, the American College of Surgeons suggests you check several items:[20]

Is the surgeon **Board Certified**? Board certification is an indication that the

---

[20] © 1996-2000. American College of Surgeons, Chicago, Ill. (http://www.facs.org/public_info/)

surgeon has completed training in the specialty and has been approved by the American Board of Medical Specialties.

Is the surgeon a **Fellow of the American College of Surgeons** (FACS)? This is an indication that the surgeon has passed a thorough evaluation by his peers. A Fellow is Board Certified in his specialty. One of the requirements is that he refrain from performing unjustified operations.

Will the surgery be performed in an **Accredited Health Care Facility**? The surgeon will have been approved to practice in one or more facilities. The facility should be accredited by the Joint Commission on Accreditation of Healthcare Organizations (JCAHO) or either the Joint Commission for, or the Accreditation Association for, Ambulatory Health Care (for outpatient surgery centers).

Another valuable resource is your state's medical society and the state's medical licensing board.

When surgery appears to be the choice, there are other questions to consider. Ask if there are any alternatives. There may be medications which will help and at least delay the need for an operation. Every operation has risks. They may be as mild as nausea or as severe as death. Before any operation is performed, at least two professionals will go through their check list, warning you of anything and everything that could happen. This is known as *informed consent.* You should ask about the real risks, those after-effects which are likely or which happen in many cases. Don't panic about those things which can happen, but rarely do.

A prime consideration in deciding on surgery is simple: Will the operation improve the patient's health or quality of life? A procedure which will prolong a patient's life but not improve the quality of that life may not be the best choice. We will discuss quality of life issues later in this book.

Finally, you need to know the immediate and long term effects of the operation. These include the projected length of any hospital stay, as well as any rehabilitation regimen.

Having told you to take your time when making a decision, you should know that there are times you cannot take the time to obtain a second opinion. Some emergencies require immediate action, such as acute appendicitis, a blood clot or aneurysm, or an accidental injury. In cases like these, the need for immediate action makes choice a luxury you cannot afford. You should preplan whenever possible. For instance, you should know your doctors of choice and your hospital of choice

Medical Tests

As the caregiver, you will accompany the patient to hospitals, clinics and doctors' offices for tests. You will want to make these trips as comfortable as possible for everyone.

First, you need to know what medicines, including over-the-counter or homeopathic remedies, the patient is taking. Keep track of them using the chart in Appendix H (page 201). Often, no medications are allowed prior to the test. This restriction may involve anything from several hours to several days. For some tests, eating is not allowed for some period of time before the test. Know the restrictions ahead of time. There is nothing so frustrating as getting to the hospital for a test, parking the car, helping the patient into the lab, and finding out they can't administer the test.

You should also keep track of the various tests administered to the patient. Use the chart in Appendix J (beginning on page 201).

Some patients may have side effects from the test or from the preparation. In those cases, you will need to stay in touch with the patient's doctor. If there is a medication given before the test, failing to take or finish that medication can be harmful or may prevent the doctor from getting the correct results.

A patient may have an allergy to the pre-test medications or to the test medications themselves. You need to know what the patient is allergic to. Allergies may include certain dyes, topical medications, or dental medications.

If the patient has any implants, involving metal usually, those implants may have an affect or may affect the ability to even have the test. If this condition exists and the facility does not want to perform the test, look for a second opinion. Some facilities may have other equipment which will allow them to proceed.

Arrive on time. Late arrival may result in the medication wearing off. You also need to plan for traffic jams, construction, car trouble or other delays. Make sure you have enough gas for the trip.

Before the test, be sure the name, address, and medical information matches the patient's. Ask what procedure being performed. This will assure that the correct test is being given to the correct person.

Following discharge, watch for side effects and reactions. There is nothing wrong with insisting that the patient remain in the waiting room, coffee shop, or other nearby area, for an hour or two to be sure there are no side effects. If preparation involved fasting, a lighter meal than usual will help the patient start back on a proper diet.

If the patient is remaining in the facility for a period of time while waiting for, or after the test, be sure to carry a list of any food allergies as well as the allergies mentioned earlier. Failing to alert the kitchen can lead to bigger problems than the one you are trying to solve.

Choking

Choking is a condition which cannot wait for emergency services. It is helpful for you to know the Heimlich Maneuver. There are different procedures depending upon the patient's age and condition. The procedures vary for infants, adults, adults in wheelchairs, and even on yourself. There are procedures outlined on eHow (www.ehow.com/how_14949_heimlich-maneuver.html)[21] and from Medline Plus (http://MedlinePlus.gov). If you want to be able to perform this procedure, do not wait until it is needed. Practice needs to be done well ahead of time.

In all cases, call 9-1-1 as soon as possible. It is always helpful to use a speaker phone so you can follow the operator's instructions while keeping your hands free.

For babies younger than one,[22] thumps on the back while the baby is held, face down, should dislodge the item. It not, thrusts on the chest may help.

Other problems with young children can include the swallowing of objects or poisons. If you are not sure whether something is poisonous, assume it is and contact 9-1-1 or the Poison Control Center immediately. If possible, have the container handy.

Watch for difficult or noisy breathing, the swallowing of any other object, like something sharp. Watch to see if anything is stuck.

---

[21] Or go to www.ehow.com/ and enter *Heimlich* in the search engine.
[22] From Healthwise, Incorporated © 2005-2007 WebMD, Inc. (www.webmd.com/)

Specific Diseases

Many diseases seem worse because the patient feels uncomfortable. The discomfort can make other conditions seem worse. Food can make a difference for many patients.

Cut down or eliminate trans fats and saturated fats. Use olive oil and polyunsaturated fats. Emphasize Omega-3 fish oil.

Eliminate or reduce refined products. Use whole grain bread rather than white bread, brown rice rather than white rice, baked potatoes rather than French fries, and eliminate soda with sugar.

Eat lots of fruits and vegetables. Raw is better than cooked for most people.

Nuts are good health foods (barring allergies), but try to avoid the salty ones.

Chocolate and alcohol are good in moderation because of the sugar content. Stick with dark chocolate. Too much chocolate leads to too much sugar. The same theory applies to alcohol. One drink can be beneficial. More can be destructive.

Spices have anti-inflammatory properties. Be careful when the patient has allergies or a queasy stomach.

Make all food adjustments slowly to avoid adverse reactions. Introduce one at a time so that, if the patient has a problem, you can easily identify its source..

There are some diseases which occur often enough and generally require a caregiver that they deserve special mention. They usually require specialized and extensive care. While we will indicate some of them, this is not meant to be a complete list. We include them here primarily so you can watch for early signs.

Cancer

Cancer is the second leading cause of death in the United States (after heart disease). There are four types of cancer which account for more than half the new cases diagnosed each year. They are: Lung, colorectal, breast, and prostate. In all cases, the best treatment is early treatment. The biggest problem with cancer is that, by the time symptoms appear, the cancer is usually advanced. Take advantage of screenings which can lead to early detection. After that, take regular steps to monitor susceptibility on a regular schedule. Doctors do not know why one person gets cancer and another doesn't.

Lung cancer is the leading cause of cancer death. The most obvious cause of lung cancer is cigarette smoke, either directly by smoking or second hand, by being exposed to smoke. Other causes include exposure to asbestos, arsenic, chromium, nickel or radon.

Some of the early signs to monitor include:
- A history of smoking
- A history of being in heavy smoke areas
- A persistent cough
- Chest discomfort
- Breathing trouble
- Wheezing
- Hoarseness
- Streaks of blood in sputum (mucus coughed up from the lungs)
- Loss of appetite
- Inexplicable weight loss
- Feelings of being constantly tired

Although testing for lung cancer does not necessarily decrease the chances of dying from the disease, knowing of its existence is the best start in control. Prompt treatment may extend a patient's life even if does not offer a cure. The two most common tests are a chest x-ray and sputum cytology (coughing up mucus and having it viewed under a microscope for cancer cells). An extensive physical examination and history is also needed. The doctor will check for lumps or anything unusual. The history will also include health habits, past jobs, illnesses, and treatments. There are other tests which are performed after the initial diagnosis, ranging from blood, urine, and tissue examinations to biopsies (where some tissue is removed and examined).

As with every test, there are risks. In addition to the exposure of radiation from the x-ray, false-positive and false-negative results can occur. Moreover, according to the government's Agency for Healthcare Research and Quality, the discovery of lung cancer may not improve the patient's health and may not help the patient live longer. It is better, however, to know what the patient is facing. Discuss with the doctor the risk for this disease and the advisability of screening tests.

The chance of recovery depends upon the type of lung cancer, the patient's general health, the type and severity of the symptoms, and the stage of the disease (the size of the tumor and whether or not it has spread to other parts of the body).

Treatment options include surgery, radiation, chemotherapy, laser therapy, photodynamic therapy, and observation.

Colorectal cancer (cancer of the colon or rectum) is the second leading cause of cancer deaths in the United States. The risk of developing this type of cancer increases after the age of 40. Current studies have shown that several factors may affect colorectal cancer risk. Some can be changed, while others cannot. Some of the risk factors include:

- Smoking
- Obesity
- Alcohol
- Lack of physical activity

- Insufficient vitamin D[23]
- Insufficient folic acid[24]

After the age of 40, most people should have a sigmoidoscopy or colonoscopy. A sigmoidoscopy allows the doctor to examine the lower colon while a colonoscopy covers the entire colon. During those examinations, the doctor will remove any polyps (growths) and have them examined for malignancy. A polyp which is removed can no longer become cancerous. A colonoscopy is suggested on a schedule ranging from one year to five years, depending upon the patient's history and the results of the previous tests.

For women, hormones can be a mixed blessing. Studies show that a combination of estrogen and progesterone lowers the risk of colorectal cancer (estrogen alone does not), but the combination increases the risk of breast cancer, blood clots, and heart disease.

Breast cancer is the second leading cause of cancer deaths in women. While breast cancer does appear in men, it is much less common. The first line of defense against breast cancer is self examination. Tell the doctor if the patient has any lumps in the breasts or if any changes are seen. The most common tests for breast cancer are a mammogram, biopsy, or a hormone test. A big part of the chance of recovery is how early the cancer is discovered.

Prostate cancer affects many men, but the majority of those who develop it do not die from it. The risk of developing prostate cancer increases with age. A patient should consult with a doctor if any of the following occur:

- Weak or interrupted urine flow

---

[23] Studies show that 1,000 units of vitamin D taken daily may cut the risk of colorectal cancer in half.
[24] High doses of folic acid may help decrease colorectal cancer risk.

- Frequent urination
- Painful urination
- Trouble urinating
- Blood in the urine or semen
- Painful ejaculation
- A pain which doesn't go away, in the back, hips, or pelvis

Tests the doctor may perform include a digital rectal exam, a PSA (Prostate-specific antigen) test, a transrectal ultrasound, or a biopsy.

As with all forms of cancer, the most important consideration is early detection. While some of the tests may seem intrusive and uncomfortable, they are not as uncomfortable as the disease itself. Cancer is a slowly progressing disease. When someone notes "how quickly" someone dies from cancer, he is merely reacting to the fact that the disease was discovered only after it had progressed to a late state, generally after several years or longer. In an elderly patient, the caregiver must weigh the possible benefits of cancer treatment against whether or not the patient's life will be extended or made more comfortable. Always discuss options with the patient's doctors.

Aftercare

There are things to watch for after cancer is discovered. Notify the patient's doctor if you notice any of the following:

- Fatigue
- Pain
- Cardiopulmonary symptoms
- Fever
- Sweating
- Hot Flashes (where none should be expected)
- Nausea
- Vomiting
- Sleep difficulty
- Anxiety

- Depression

Pain can be controlled. If the Oncologist cannot relieve the pain, ask to see a pain control specialist. If all else fails, the National Cancer Institutes[25] can put you in touch with pain management facilities.

Fatigue is one of the most common side effects and may last from days or weeks to months or even years.

Take your time. While some people can return to former activities almost immediately, others need time to recuperate sufficiently. Each patient is different. Everyone recovers at a different rate.

Support groups can be valuable not only for the patient, but for the caregiver. Groups can meet at hospitals, churches, or even over the internet. Make the effort to find a group which is helpful and appropriate for your patient and for you. They don't need to be the same group.

Respite care is essential. You cannot and should not be an active caregiver all day, every day. You need an occasional break. Call upon family, friends, neighbors, non-profit groups, government agencies, or volunteers.

Exercise is important both for you and the patient. Any exercise is acceptable, even just walking around the block. As with all changes in regimen, consult with your doctor for instructions and limitations.

A normal side effect of cancer is loss of **Weight** caused by a loss of appetite. A patient will often lose the will to eat. On the other side, the sedentary life common after a major illness may lead to weight gain. Neither is desired.

If your patient is a **child**, the care may be similar, but your actions may not be. Explain

---

[25] National Cancer Institutes is a government agency, part of the National Institutes of Health. (www.cancer.gov) or 1-800-4-CANCER.

that you will still be there to care for him and, even though he is better, you may feel bad and it may take some time for you to feel better. Also make it clear that you will make sure he attends all the doctor appointments.

Heart Attack[26]

Coronary heart disease is the number one killer in America. More than 25 percent of the deaths in the U.S. are from heart disease. If your patient displays these symptoms, do NOT take her to the hospital. Call 9-1-1 immediately. **NEVER** let the patient drive herself to the hospital. While it may take a few minutes for an ambulance to arrive, paramedics are equipped to provide on-site emergency care.

An Illustration

Beverly fell on the kitchen floor. Elderly and frail, she could not get up. Her husband, Carl, picked her up, carried her to his car, and drove her to the hospital, only several miles away. He felt that the ride would be faster than waiting for an ambulance. Unfortunately, because of the way he picked Beverly up, she fractured her hip. The hospital told Carl that Beverly suffers from osteoporosis (weak bones) and was particularly susceptible.

While it may take some time for an ambulance to arrive, the time from the initial attack to receiving some medical help is generally much faster when you wait for the ambulance. The attendants are trained to give immediate aid and can also react

---

26 Portions excerpted from the American Heart Association (www.americanheart.org) © 2007 and MedlinePlus (an arm of the Government's Institutes of Health)

appropriately to things which may arise during transport. The same rule applies to driving yourself to a hospital. Always call 9-1-1 in an emergency.

The symptoms of a heart attack do not appear suddenly (unlike cardiac arrest, which can be fatal if not treated immediately). Most start slowly with mild pain or discomfort. It is often attributed incorrectly to an upset stomach or a bit of chest pain that may go away after a few minutes. Don't take the chance. It is better to call an ambulance and find that it was not needed than to not call one when you should have. When a patient tells you it's nothing, don't listen. In addition, she will receive faster care if she arrives in an ambulance rather than in your car.

Some of the signs you should watch for include:

- Chest discomfort
- Uncomfortable pressure, squeezing, fullness, or pain in the chest
- Upper body discomfort in one or both arms, back, neck, jaw or stomach
- Shortness of breath
- Cold sweat
- Nausea
- Lightheadedness

Not every symptom occurs in every case.

To assess the care the patient receives, she should receive regular blood pressure measurements and cholesterol testing. The doctors and nurses should be checking these frequently. Once released from the hospital, you should learn when and how to monitor pulse and blood pressure.

There are some things which can affect normal readings. Before taking the patient's blood pressure, make sure she has not had caffeine or cigarettes for at least 30 minutes. Be sure she has used the bathroom (a full bladder can affect the result). Use a straight-backed chair if possible. Have her keep her feet flat on the floor for at least five minutes. Rest her arm on a table at heart level.

Other factors which affect the reading are sleep, time of day, exercise, some medications, some herbal supplements, some foods (especially licorice), and stress. Sometimes, blood pressure spikes when the patient is around the doctor (called White-Coat Hypertension).

Try to take blood pressure readings at the same time or times every day. If there are wild fluctuations, notify the doctor. He may want to consider a 24-hour monitoring test.

Immediately after a heart attack, aspirin is usually prescribed. You should ask the 9-1-1 operator if you should have the patient take an aspirin immediately and, if so, how much. Be sure to tell the operator about any allergies the patient may have.

Aftercare

To help prevent or minimize heart disease, try to have the patient exercise regularly, refrain from smoking, keep track of her blood pressure and cholesterol levels, have her eat fruits and vegetables, and keep her weight in check (consult with the doctor to be sure there is no down side to this regimen).

After a heart attack, there are steps you should take as caregiver. You need to encourage the patient in several ways:

Lower cholesterol: the latest studies by the American Heart Association and the American College of Cardiology suggest the lower the LDL (the bad cholesterol), the better. The target is now 70 mg/dL or less. That is a very difficult level to achieve and may require medication.

Lower blood pressure: The patient should aim for a blood pressure below 140/90. With the addition of diabetes or chronic kidney disease, a target under 130/80 is recommended. Although healthy eating, weight control, moderate (only) alcohol use, and exercise are the first steps, medications may be necessary.

Smoking: As mentioned in several places throughout this book, smoking and the proximity to second-hand smoke are extremely unhealthy. Smoking cessation programs are readily available as are other techniques. Make sure no one else smokes around the patient.

Weight: The patient's body mass index[27] should be between 18.5 and 24.9. A waistline 40 inches or less for a man, and 35 or less for a woman is recommended.

Diabetes management: Keep the hemoglobin A_1c under seven percent. Ask the doctor if periodic testing is warranted.

Aspirin therapy: A low dose of aspirin daily is generally appropriate. In addition, some people require prescription medication.

Flu vaccine: Most doctors recommend a flu shot every year, as well as the pneumonia vaccine shot.

Other medications: In some cases a beta blocker, or ACE inhibitor may be helpful to those with heart problems. As with all items, always check with the patient's doctors before adopting any steps.

Stroke

Stroke, the third leading cause of death, is similar in symptoms to a heart attack. Immediate care by a trained professional is required. According to the American Stroke Association, "Time lost is brain lost." The warning signs of a stroke are:

---

[27] To compute the body mass index, multiply the patient's weight by 703. Divide that answer by the patient's height in inches squared (inches times inches).

- Sudden numbness or weakness of the face, arm or leg
- Sudden confusion
- Trouble speaking or understanding
- Trouble seeing in one or both eyes
- Sudden trouble walking
- Difficulty writing
- Dizziness
- Loss of balance or coordination
- Sudden, severe headache with no known cause

To help recognize the trouble signs, remember the acronym, FAST. Consider the patient's face, arms and speech, while remembering that time is critical.

Keep track of the time and when the symptoms first appear. In some cases, some clot-busting drugs can reduce long-term disabilities. There is currently no way to reverse the effects of a stroke, but it is important to prevent further strokes.

Aftercare

As a caregiver, your primary job after a stroke is to keep the patient's spirits up. Rehabilitation is hard but necessary work. If she is able to return home, you should expect to spend more time with her. Don't talk down to the patient and don't talk to others as if the patient is not there.

If the patient has trouble communicating, ask for an assessment by a speech/language pathologist.

Ask for permission to attend some of the rehabilitation sessions. You will learn what is being done and how you can help. You will also learn how to encourage the patient to practice the skills she learns in rehabilitation sessions.

Find out if there is any special equipment which will needed. Some equipment which may be indicated includes a cane, walker, braces, wheelchair, bathtub grab bars and floor mats, communication aids, and Velcro fasteners for clothes. If appropriate, help the patient explore work, volunteer opportunities, or adult daycare.

Ask about proper clothing as well as appropriate shoes and sneakers for the patient.

Keep close tabs on medication schedules, as well as exercise, diet and rest instructions.

Don't be afraid to ask for help. You should look for friends or family members to stay with the patient so you can get an occasional break. Don't neglect such supports as Meals on Wheels, home health agencies, Visiting Nurses Associations, and adult day care facilities. Also, there are support groups available as well as a variety of professional resources. A good start would be the American Heart Association.

Cardiac Arrest

Cardiac arrest strikes immediately and without warning. Signs include:

- Sudden loss of responsiveness
- No normal breathing

To check for cardiac arrest, tap the patient on the shoulder. If there is no response, call 9-1-1 immediately and begin CPR, if you are qualified. (As a caregiver, you should strongly consider becoming certified in CPR. Contact your local office of the American Red Cross for locally available classes.)

If you tilt the patient's head up, he should take a normal breath. Give him at least five seconds. If there is no reaction, call 9-1-1 and begin CPR.

Aftercare

Cardiac arrest has many of the same symptoms as a heart attack. The aftercare program is similar. Monitoring of cholesterol, weight, blood pressure, and smoking are all important. Don't let the patient sit around the house and do nothing.

Diabetes

Diabetes affects more than one out of every 16 people in the country. It also increases the risk for blindness, kidney disease, heart disease and strokes. If your patient suffers from diabetes, make sure that she receives regular blood glucose and cholesterol tests. She should also have yearly eye exams and flu shots. The services of a podiatrist may be advisable for year-round foot care.

Aftercare

After diabetes is diagnosed, control and monitoring are most important. Depending upon the severity, the doctor may prescribe anything from injections to oral medications to diet. The doctor may also recommend regular testing of blood sugar levels.

A **healthy diet** is most important. If necessary, take the patient to a registered dietitian. Obesity has also been shown to be a major contributor to diabetes. In some cases, losing weight will cause the diabetes to disappear. A diet high in fiber and low in sugar is desirable.

Schedule meals at the same time each day. This will allow the doctor to prescribe the correct dose of insulin and will help keep blood sugar levels even.

Exercise is an important component. Any exercise is better than nothing. Even as little as 20 minutes of walking three times each week has been shown to be beneficial.

Dementia

Dementia is a catch-all for symptoms caused by disorders of the brain. The most well-known condition is Alzheimer's disease. The patient may have trouble doing many things properly, such as getting dressed, eating, solving problems, having language be understood, controlling emotions or remembering people or things. Those with dementia have serious problems with two or more of these, such as memory and language.

Memory loss by itself is not proof of dementia. The condition is not sudden. Generally, your patient will not show the signs of dementia overnight. It occurs slowly, possibly starting with some forgetfulness, but not about everything. The patient may not be aware of the problem.

There are several medications available to treat some forms of dementia. The good news is they may slow down the disease or improve the symptoms. The other news is they can't cure the diseases. Slowing the disease down is not necessarily a good thing, however. As a care-giver, you need to consider the "quality of life" issue when discussing the medications and options with the patient's doctors.

In addition to Alzheimer's disease, some causes of dementia can include a head injury, stroke or brain tumor. A family history of dementia should also be considered.

An Illustration

Michael started screaming from his bed in a local nursing home, insisting that his wastebasket was on fire. His daughter, who was in the hall, raced to the nursing station to alert the staff. The nurse on duty nodded and went to Michael's room where she showed Michael's daughter that there was, in fact, no fire. "That's the Alzheimer's," the nurse said quietly.

When a patient has dementia, check out any reports, if you can do so quickly and safely, before rushing for help. Pay attention but don't panic.

You should watch for some of these signs:
- Memory loss
- Forgetting simple words
- Using the wrong words

- Cooking a meal but forgetting to serve it
- Forgetting that she cooked a meal
- Neglecting personal safety or hygiene
- Asking the same question and not remembering she asked it moments earlier
- Forgetting where she is, even on the same street
- Forgetting simple things
- Forgetting how to enter items in a checkbook
- Putting things in the wrong places
- Forgetting where things were put
- Inability to follow directions
- Frequent mood swings
- Losing the desire to go places she once liked
- Irritability
- Suspicion

Showing some of these symptoms is not necessarily a sign of dementia. You should look for repeated instances of multiple symptoms. Some of these items are natural signs of aging. Some don't even require aging. We all forget an occasional appointment.

You can slow down the onset of dementia by keeping the patient active. Exercise for the brain may include doing the daily crossword or Sudoku, taking a class, learn to operate a computer, learn a language, or spend time with other people in conversation.

Some causes of dementia which can be "cured" are those caused by things you can control: dehydration, poor nutrition, bad reactions to medication, thyroid problems which can be controlled with medication, minor head injuries, and high fevers. These are treatable.

There are other steps you can take, especially in the early stages of dementia. Compensation can include making a list of things to do and using other memory aids, such as calendars and notes. Keep the patient's mind as active as possible with hobbies or interests which will be stimulating. Dementia involves the damage of brain cells. Once destroyed, brain cells cannot be replaced or regenerated.

There are treatments, although at this time the available treatments can slow the progression of the disease, but not cure it.

Consult with the doctor as early as possible. There are tests available to determine if your patient has dementia. You should ask your primary physician to refer you to a specialist in geriatrics.

Aftercare

Avoid situations which lead to **frustration**. For example, if the patient has difficulty dressing, don't expect the patient to get dressed without assistance. Have her put on one item alone, like a jacket.

Choose the "right" times. Save more difficult tasks for times when she appears more calm.

Encourage good **sleep habits**. The patient may have trouble knowing when it is daytime and when it is nighttime. Keep the curtains open and a clock which can be seen easily. Limit or eliminate caffeine intake. Discourage naps. Encourage exercise during the day. Keep the bedroom quiet. Use a nightlight.

You need to watch for **wandering**. Dementia patients tend to wander and then forget where they are or where they live. Make sure the patient is wearing an identification bracelet. Have a plan in place. You can speak with the local police department and the patient's doctors for information on who to call or how you might set up an alert system. You might need locks on some doors or an alarm system on the bed.

An Illustration

Dennis, a strong and healthy senior citizen, got up one morning, kissed his wife and told her he was going to the airport. Although his wife knew that he had been getting confused and that he had no one to pick up at the airport, she could not stop him. When he left, she immediately called the police and explained the situation. The police stopped Dennis on the highway, had an ambulance transport him to the hospital. The emergency room ran tests and discovered that Dennis had suffered from a stroke.

Quick thinking and positive action can save the life of a loved one.

A Final Word

It is inevitable that your time as a caregiver will end. If you are a caregiver to a young child, that child will grow older, more self-reliant and able to make his own way in the world. If you have done your job well, you will be remembered and revered.

If you are the caregiver to a person temporarily disabled by an accident or severe illness, she will improve and no longer require the commitment you have made, although you should be remembered fondly.

If you are caregiver to an elderly or totally disabled person, be prepared for the next step in the evolution of your patient. Some patients die quietly at home. That presents an entirely new set of conditions. For assistance in that area, turn to Section IV (page 119). In other cases, the patient's condition deteriorates beyond your capability (or anyone's capability) to cope with the overwhelming responsibility of continuing and increasing care. At that point, the patient requires a higher level of care, which can be in a hospital, hospice, nursing home, assisted-living facility, rehabilitation facility, or retirement facility.

This does not end your tenure as caregiver, but it does change it. In the next section, the discussion provides topics such as selecting the best facility, dealing with the professionals in that facility, and interacting with the staff. You may also refer back to portions of this section to review information on medication (page 67), medical tests (page 76), and surgery (page 73).

Section III - In-Patient Care

Once you have determined that your patient requires more care than you can give at home, you should understand that you haven't done anything wrong, improper, or bad. The need for a higher level of care than you can give at home is natural. Some patients require that higher level earlier than others. You will continue to have the primary responsibility to assure the best care possible.

Location

The first job as caregiver is to determine which type of care will best fit the patient. Part of that investigation involves the location. If at all possible, the location of the facility should be such that family and friends can easily visit.

Rehabilitation facility - A short term option to restore abilities after a major illness or accident.

Rest Home - A facility which provides housing and general care for the elderly and the convalescent.

Nursing Home - A privately of publicly owned and operated facility for people unable to care for themselves properly, such as the aged or chronically ill. Those in a nursing home generally require a higher level of care and assistance than you can provide at home.

Hospice - A facility or program to provide for the physical and emotional needs of the terminally ill. Hospice care can be provided at home or in a facility.

Hospital - The highest level of care possible. Most, if not all, insurance companies want to get the patient out of the hospital as quickly as possible since the hospital has the highest cost.

Rehabilitation Facility

Rehabilitation is a temporary arrangement. It can include care from a physical therapist, occupational therapist, speech and language pathologist, or physiatrist (specialist in physical medicine and rehabilitation), among others. The patient may have used the services of one or more professionals in an at-home or outpatient situation. There are also a variety of organizations ready to assist in locating a facility where more intensive care can be offered. Organizations associated with a particular disease (for example, multiple sclerosis, cancer, stroke) can offer assistance. The patient's primary doctor can also suggest specialists or agencies that can help. When you are considering a facility, ask whether the facility specializes in conditions the patient has. Each of the professionals should be certified. Also ask if the facility offers 24-hour care, if that will be needed. Generally, the patient will be sent to a more permanent facility within four to twelve weeks.

The settings you will research can be nursing homes with a rehabilitation unit, a stand-alone rehabilitation hospital or center, or a special unit within a traditional hospital setting. Check with sources of accreditation of facilities in your state. You can talk to the state ombudsman, investigate lawsuits, and look at the paperwork each facility must maintain about violations and corrective actions.

Assisted Living Facility

There are facilities which combine the benefits of nursing care with the benefit of an attached rehabilitation program. They are usually short term but may be the perfect place for someone who is unable to care for herself but is not quite ready for full time care.

Rest Home

A rest home generally offers the least degree of personalized care. If you were providing care in your home, a rest home may not be an improvement. As caregiver, you are probably providing a higher level of care than your patient would receive from a rest home. A rest home is closer to a retirement community than it is to an assisted living facility.

Hospital

If your patient requires a hospital, he has either suffered an injury or an acute illness, or requires diagnostic testing. A hospital will provide urgent care for a short period of time. Because of insurance rules, regardless of whether or not a specific rule applies to him, the hospital will try to discharge the patient as quickly as possible, sometimes before they should. Don't be afraid to voice your opinion if you do not feel that the patient is ready to be discharged. Enlist his primary care physician in this discussion. (If the patient's primary care physician is not willing to work with you, it may be time to find another.) Appeals are always available.

An important part of discharge is determining the appropriate next step. Do not let the hospital discharge a patient with nowhere to go. It is not your responsibility as caregiver to find the next facility, nor is it your job to transport the patient to that facility. If the patient requires a nursing home, for instance, it is the hospital's job to find an appropriate facility and to arrange for transportation to that facility. While the hospital will often insist that the patient cannot stay at the hospital, it is unreasonable to expect him to be on the street.

Never allow the hospital, or any other facility, to put you in a position you cannot handle appropriately.

Hospice

An in-patient hospice facility is for the patient who requires extensive, specialized care, usually with pain management. Generally, it is a final-stage facility, offering pain relief and symptom control (called palliative care), rather than trying to effect a cure. The hospice will have a full staff of physicians, nurses, social workers, counselors, nursing assistants, clergy, therapists and volunteers. They also provide medication, supplies, equipment and hospital-type services.[28]

As with most other types of care, check with the patient's insurance carrier for infor-

---

[28] For more information or to find a hospice facility near you, see www.caringinfo.org or call the National Hospice Helpline toll-free at 1-800-658-8898.

mation about coverage. Medicare and the majority of Medicaid and private insurance companies offer coverage. Ask about what co-payments may be required.

During the early days of hospice stay, most of the time will be spent by the staff doing assessments. After the first several weeks, you will be asked to spend time with the patient, although volunteers may assist with errands and to provide a break.

If a patient shows a marked improvement or remission of symptoms, the hospice may transfer her back home or to a nursing home.

Most hospices also have bereavement groups to offer support after death.

Patient Bill of Rights

In 1998, the government adopted a patient bill of rights for Medicare and Medicaid (the Government-sponsored insurance program for low-income) patients. Since that time, many facilities either have adopted these rights or have adopted their own similar list. There are three goals of the program:

First, to strengthen consumer confidence that the health care system is fair and responsive;

Second, to reaffirm the importance of a strong relationship between patients and health care providers; and

Finally, to reaffirm the critical role the patient (and the caregiver) play in safeguarding health.

The bill of rights has these principles:
- **The right to information**
    The patient has the right to receive accurate, easy to understand information to assist in making appropriate medical decisions. She and you are also entitled to know when treatment is or will be provided by students, interns,

residents, or other trainees. All providers should also introduce themselves.

- **The right of choice**

  The patient has the right to choose providers, specialists, and facilities to assure the highest quality care possible. According to Medicare, medically necessary services must be available 24 hours a day, seven days a week. The patient and you also need to understand the benefits and risks of each treatment option and whether a particular treatment is experimental or part of a research study. If a treatment option is experimental, or if the insurance companies believes it is, it may affect out-of-pocket costs. Most insurance companies will not cover experimental treatments.

- **Access to emergency services**

  If a patient has severe pain, acute symptoms, a sudden illness, or an injury, she has the right to emergency health service. Federal law prohibits all hospitals from denying such services regardless of the ability to pay. Health plans must provide this service without need for a preauthorization, even if normally there is a gatekeeper[29] in the plan.

- **Participation in decisions**

  A patient has the right to participate fully in all decisions related to health care. You, as caregiver, should be designated to act and be consulted in her place. This designation is accomplished by a Power of Attorney. Health plan contracts should not contain a gag clause,

---

[29] The general term *gatekeeper* refers to the primary physician in many plans who is responsible for issuing and approving referrals to most specialists.

preventing a professional from discussing and advising the patient or you about all medically necessary treatment options. Treatment options may also include "no treatment." This paragraph is known as *informed consent*. The rules also provide that physicians must disclose to Medicare and Medicaid patients any arrangements that give them a financial incentive to limit care. Don't be afraid to ask about such financial incentives.

- **Non-discrimination**

  The patient and you have the right to be treated with consideration and respect from all health care professionals. She should not be discriminated against because of race, ethnicity, national origin, religion, sex, age, disability, sexual orientation, genetic information, payment source or the ability to pay for care.

- **Confidentiality**

  The patient and you have the right to communicate with health care providers and be assured that the information will be kept in strict confidence. Without a court order or subpoena, unauthorized persons are not allowed access to the patient's records. You also have the right to review and copy medical records and, if you find anything which is not accurate, relevant, or complete, ask the doctor or facility to change that record. Make your request in writing. Recheck the files to be certain changes were made.

- **Complaints**

  When you or your patient disagrees with the health plan, provider, or facility, you and she have the right to a fair, fast and objective review. The review may not be done by anyone involved in the first decision. Most hospitals and insurance companies have a review procedure in place. You are always entitled to this independent review. This review can cover everything from the waiting time for a procedure to the operating hours of the facility, the adequacy of the facility, or even the conduct of the care providers.

- **Your responsibility**

    As part of the bill of rights, the government commission recognized that a patient also has the responsibility for maintaining good health as much as possible. That can be interpreted to mean that she must eat appropriately, take medication as prescribed, and try not to do anything she knows will adversely affect her health.

Nursing Home

A nursing home is the most common next step after home care. It is not necessarily for elderly people alone, but rather for those who can no longer be cared for at home. In most cases, nursing care is available 24 hours a day.

As with all aspects of caregiving, you need to do your homework. The first step is to determine the type of nursing home the patient requires. The nursing home will be under the care of physicians who visit regularly and are on-call around the clock. The patient's doctor certifies the need for nursing care and can also serve as a resource. The nursing home staff and doctor will help determine the patient's care plan. Make sure the nursing home specializes or works closely with residents who require care similar to that which your patient requires.

Most of this research can be done on the phone. Start with the agencies which license and accredit agencies in your state. If the nursing home sounds like a good match on the phone, make an appointment for a tour. Visit at various times of the day so that you can get a complete picture. If possible, speak with some of the residents, provided that they are competent, and ask if they are happy and if they feel the home meets all of their needs. Also try to speak with some of their families.

An important question concerns availability. Does the nursing home have beds available? If not, the rest of the search is immaterial, unless you are planning ahead.

You also need to learn the rules. For example, many nursing homes have rules prohibiting the acceptance of gifts, even small gifts at holiday times. A better option might be to write a note to the chief executive of the facility and send copies to the appropriate nursing and other staff.

Financial considerations

Nursing home care is not inexpensive. Medicare will pay for only 20 days in full and up to 100 days partially. Medicare will not pay for long term or custodial care. Medicaid will pay after that if the patient has no assets. Medicaid is a State-Federal partnership. Most of the rules are set by the state. You can find specific rules from your state which apply to your loved one. Before Medicaid kicks in, the patient will be expected to pay from her assets until they have been depleted. That is called a spend-down. Real estate is computed by several rules. Medicaid financial planning may involve the divesting of real property. There are many parts to these rules.[30] If property is sold,

---

[30] These rules are accurate with the understanding that rules vary by state. Always check with your state because both the states and the federal government update rules and guidelines on a regular basis.

it usually must be sold at fair market value. Also, there is a period known as "look back." This minimum three-year period (up to five years in some cases) is the time during which the state may count the value of the property even though it has been sold. Consult with an attorney or financial planner early in the process.

If the patient is in a nursing home being paid for under Medicaid rules (some states may use other names, but the program is still Medicaid), the law provides for a personal needs allowance ranging from $30 to $70 per month, depending upon the state.

If she is young enough and healthy enough, the patient can buy nursing home insurance which will pay either all or part of the bill. If there is a possibility that you will become a caregiver in the near future, the likelihood is that it's too late for private insurance.

While Medicaid must provide a placement, you have virtually no choice about the location of the facility. You can, and should, appeal any decision if the nursing home with an available bed is too far away for the patient to have family and friends visit or if the patient's specialists are too far away for appropriate medical care.

Do not feel guilty about placing the patient in a nursing home. Despite earlier promises you may have made (and they are made often), things change. While you may have had the intention of never putting her in a nursing home, it is sometimes the best or only choice. Care you might have provided ten years earlier may not be possible now.

Don't feel guilty. The full time, trained staff can care for her better and more efficiently than you could. The phrase you should use is, "Your conditions now requires around the clock care I can't provide."

Ask questions

When you are researching nursing homes, keep in mind the following:

- Cost
  - What is not covered in the basic rates?
  - Does the home have Medicaid beds available?
- Services
  - Special diets
  - Beautician and hair cutting
  - Dental and podiatry services
  - Shopping trips
  - Other activities
- Location
  - Close enough for friends
  - Close enough for family
  - Near a good hospital
- Atmosphere
  - Clean and attractive
- Religious
  - Regular services
  - Clergy visits
- Medical
  - Professionals (other than the primary doctor)
  - Prescription handling
  - Therapies
  - Nearby hospital
- Caregiver role
  - Involved in the entire process
  - Frequent visits allowed
  - Helping with transition
  - Consulted for all problems and decisions
- Room considerations
  - Telephone
  - Roommate selection
  - Room decorations
  - Television
  - Heating and cooling for proper temperature control
  - Storage of personal items

Finally, you should be sure that the home has a quality assurance program and that it is certified properly. Your state should have a list of licensed and Medicare/Medicaid approved facilities.

Despite all the State oversight, licensing procedures for the facility, and licensing requirements for the staff, some nursing homes, after meeting or surpassing all the rules and requirements, are deficient.

An Illustration

Victor was living in a nursing home. After he fell out of bed twice, the doctor ordered that his bed have safety rails installed. The nursing home refused to comply. Victor fell out of bed twice more, fracturing his hip and leg. When Victor died from complications of his fractures, the death certificate listed as cause of death "accidental."

Don't trust a nursing home to provide all the care which is required. You must be vigilant at all times and don't accept the Nursing Home's story or explanation too quickly. Investigate.

Settle in

Entering a nursing home can be traumatic. **Bring some things from home** (pictures, greeting cards, chair). Provide photos. Put in a television and telephone, preferably with a direct phone number. Supply books and magazines. Encourage hobbies. If there is a telephone, whether you put it there or not, put restrictions on the phone. Ask the phone company to block long distance calls. If the phone has measured service, block all outgoing calls except to toll-free numbers. A good option may be to provide a phone card. Failure to take these steps may result in some surprising phone bills, with charges incurred by people other than your loved one.

Label everything. Every piece of clothing should have a label with the patient's name, including shoes, slippers and property. There are outlets where you can buy cloth labels to sew in. Some permanent markers may do if you test it first. In addition, make certain the home provides a written inventory, keep your own copy and update it for every change.

If the patient is capable, ask the home if you can **take her to lunch** or for a drive. The break will be good for her, and for you. Make sure the staff knows when you are expected to return. Also check the medication schedule and any dietary restrictions.

Get to **know the staff**. Most of them will be very helpful and will meet and exceed the patient's hopes and expectations.

Encourage friends and family to send **mail**. In addition to keeping the patient connected to the community, cards and letters become decorations.

The patient's **diet** will be determined by health considerations and any restrictions. Discuss with the staff any changes or treats which you would like to give her. Also make sure the staff knows if there are any foods she does not like or if she needs help eating. Equally important, remind the staff and everyone else who interacts with the patient about any allergies.

Medications

It is important to remember that nursing homes are usually short staffed and always busy. That is not an excuse for missing medications.

An Illustration

Zack was on heart medication, which he normally took each morning. When his son arrived for a visit, Zack mentioned that he had not received his medications that morning. The nurse confirmed his story and mentioned that the pharmacy "ran out" and that more was on order. The nurse added that it would be administered soon. By eight o'clock that evening, the drug had still not been administered. The nurse said the medicine would be delivered in the morning. Zack's son immediately complained to the nursing home's chief administrator and insisted that the drug be ordered immediately from an outside pharmacy. The administrator reluctantly agreed.

Every patient is entitled to receive necessary medications when they are scheduled. Don't let anyone make excuses to avoid doing what needs to be done.

It is the responsibility of the nursing home to maintain an adequate supply of every medication required for their patients. If their pharmacy runs out and they do not have a sufficient quantity to administer on the doctor's schedule, it is their responsibility to obtain the medication elsewhere, at their expense if necessary.

Trust your own judgment and appeal to whatever authority is required when you objectively believe that action is necessary.

Complaints

Don't ignore the patient's complaints, no matter how trivial they may seem. Small complaints tend to escalate into major problems if not addressed or acknowledged. In some cases, your listening alone will comfort her. Don't get upset and don't belittle her complaint.

If the complaint seems justified, discuss it with the staff. Minor complaints can be handled quickly and solved with little effort.

If the complaint is major or if you get no results, speak with the administrator. If the problem still goes unresolved or is repeated constantly, contact the ombudsman in your state. Federal law provides that each state have an ombudsman (or more than one) whose job it is to address your concerns. They usually obtain satisfactory results.

Consider Options

Often, facilities will want to discharge the patient back to your home. Sometimes, this may be practical. Often it is not.

Most facilities have a waiting list. Therefore, there is no overriding reason for them to keep a patient. Additionally, insurance companies exert enormous pressure to discharge patients as quickly as possible. They, and the facilities, have utilization review committees who set policies that dictate the earliest possible discharge. Discharge guidelines are set depending on the illness, not necessarily the needs of an individual patient.

An Illustration

Nancy had an accident in her home. She was hospitalized with many bruises and several broken bones. After several days in the hospital, Nancy was sent to a rehabilitation facility. Three days later, her husband was told that Nancy was being discharged because she was "well enough to go home." Her husband calmly and clearly appealed the decision. Part of the appeal was that the home was a two story building and that Nancy was not able to negotiate the stairs. In addition, he felt that Nancy was totally helpless, unable to manage the crutches she had been given, and still suffering from weakness and pain. Further, her husband did not feel capable of providing the care Nancy required. Her husband finally contacted the office of the head administrator and Nancy was allowed to remain in rehabilitation until she was able to negotiate the house properly and safely.

Just because they say so does not make it true that a patient can be released. Use common sense and do not be afraid to appeal as far up the ladder as necessary. This is true of hospitalization as well.

You don't always have choices but you can always make a reasonable argument when considering the option of home treatment or institutional treatment. Talk with the patient's doctors. Don't be afraid to ask why he should be released. If it is only because of insurance considerations, do not accept that decision. Your appeal can be to the doctor, a second medical opinion, other staff, facility administrator, state ombudsman, and the insurance company. The ultimate argument occurs when you refuse to accept the patient back into the home. Since he can't be put out on the street, the facility is forced to keep him or find alternatives.

As with everything else, there are always options in providing for the care of your patient. An important area to remember concerns what to do when an insurance claim is denied. Always challenge what you believe to be an improper denial. If the company's reasons are not clear, call the company and have them explain the action. Then, ask for a formal review. Finally, if the company is not willing to reconsider, contact your State insurance department.

Visiting

When family and friends visit, they are sometimes surprised by the differences in the patient from what they remember. When a patient begins to lose interest or the ability to care for himself, the result can be a shock to those who may not have seen the patient in recent times. The patient may show indications of confusion, memory loss, or a failure to exercise good judgment.

Reassure the visitors that their company is appreciated. Often, the radical change a visitor may see is the result of the condition, aging, normal deterioration, surgery, treatments, depression, medication or medication overuse, or dementia. You might want to prepare a visitor who has not seen the patient recently about what to expect. You should also encourage visitors. They are valuable both for the visitor and for the patient.

If you see any behaviors which would seem a radical change in the patient, make written notes and notify the doctors or nurses immediately. The symptoms may signal the need for medical or psychological intervention. A weekend or holiday should not be considered a reason to delay action if you are concerned.

Some changes in behavior may be the result of a medication overdose. In the proper dose, the medication is designed to alleviate a symptom, cure an illness, or make a patient more comfortable. An overdose, however, can cause hallucinations, dizziness, mood swings, depression, excessive fatigue, hyperactivities, or difficulty walking (beyond what may have become "normal"). Ask the pharmacist about what the side effects might be for a particular medication and how a drug can interact with something else the patient is taking. Not eating enough or not taking in adequate fluids can also cause disturbances.

A visitor may see what appears to be a drastic change in the patient. You can use that reaction to gauge whether or not the patient's status needs to be reported.

If a visitor is ill or doesn't feel right, ask them to stay home. Most patients are weak and highly susceptible. Not having the visitor is preferable to catching someone else's cold or infection. Ask the guest to visit another time.

Prepay Expenses

When the patient wants to prepay for funeral and other final expenses, her intent is to eliminate work and trauma. The expenses which are often the subject of prepayment include nursing homes, funerals, gravesites and headstones.

The prepayment of **nursing home** expenses involves an insurance policy which is inexpensive if purchased young in life and more expensive as she ages. We have covered that in detail earlier.

Prepayment for **funeral** expenses involves the purchase of a single payment annuity with the funeral home as beneficiary. The patient pays the current rate for the funeral and the home purchases an annuity from an insurance company. The interest earned by the annuity covers the yearly increase in the cost of the funeral. The funeral director may try to tell you that the interest does not cover the increase in the cost. That is nothing but a sales pitch. The funeral home has already agreed to accept the annuity as payment in full.

Paperwork is everything. You must know exactly what is covered. Usually, the policy will cover the clergyperson's gratuity, use of the chapel, organ, casket, hearse, family cars, newspaper announcement, and the opening of the grave. It will not cover overtime if the grave must be opened on a weekend or if snow needs to be cleared in the cemetery. The patient or you can include or exclude any aspect of the contract at the time of purchase.

Some **casket** companies have begun marketing directly to consumers at discount prices. Don't let the funeral home tell you that you can't buy your own.

Some people don't want the chapel, preferring a grave-side service only. Others may opt for cremation.

The **newspaper** announcement is a paid advertisement. The contract usually provides only for a local newspaper. Announcements in additional papers will incur further charges.

The number of **family cars** should be determined by the number of people in the patient's immediate family who need transportation. Remember that additional charges will be made at then current rates, while reductions will often be made at the rate listed on the original contract. Other additional charges may accrue if you move to another city or a different nearby state.

If you are involved in the original purchase of a prepaid funeral plan, check on the insurance company. Ask the state and the Better Business Bureau (at the very least) about the company and its likelihood of still being in existence and solvent when you need them. Make sure the beneficiary is transferable. If you move with the patient to another area, you don't necessarily want to be locked in to what will then be a distant funeral home. If you do move, consult with the local funeral home to be sure they will accept the value of the annuity as payment in full.

The cost of a **gravesite** does not include the burial expense or the headstone. If you are affiliated with a house of worship, they may own a cemetery for members. You should also consider the extra expense known as perpetual care. That will include the cost of maintaining the grounds and gravesite.

Headstones can be contracted for ahead of time from a monument company. Beware that you will not be at the top of the list since they have already been paid. Made sure all the engraving instructions are in writing. Double and triple check the spelling of everything. The only thing that should be missing is the date of death. The location of that information should be indicated.

If everything is prepaid, the only items you will need to pay for are additional family cars, excess travel if either you have moved or the death takes place outside the area, additional newspaper advertisements, clearing of snow and ice at the cemetery and the opening of the grave if it needs to be done on a weekend or holiday. If the death occurs outside the area, a local funeral home will be contacted. They will arrange to ship the body to the appropriate airport. Additional expenses will be incurred. The local home must be notified immediately that burial will take place in another state. Caskets are high on the priority list for airline shipments, but there may be other pitfalls. For instance, in Florida, a body which will be transported out of state must be refrigerated within 24 hours of death.

Final Wishes

No one likes to discuss his own mortality, but it is necessary. You should have completed a Power of Attorney and a Living Will for the person in your care. Those documents have been discussed earlier. One of the more common requests is a DNR order (Do Not Resuscitate). However, a DNR is not automatic and is not without choices which must be addressed by you in writing.

During surgery, a patient's heart might stop. Resuscitation in that case might allow for full recovery with no aftereffects. In that case, you would certainly want the doctors to resuscitate. In other cases, the patient might be on a feeding tube, beyond all medical hope, in a coma, or on full life support. The chance of any recovery might be non-existent. In such a case, a DNR order makes sense. You should discuss with the patient the various scenarios which might occur so you can act as he would have wished. This task requires a high level of tact.

An Illustration

Phyllis was living in a nursing home. Because of her advanced diabetes, both legs had been amputated. Her records indicated that she should not be resuscitated and that no extraordinary methods should be employed to keep her alive. Nothing should be given except for pain. One night, she complained of pain and was taken to the hospital, where it was determined that she had a bowel obstruction. Despite the orders, the hospital operated to remove the obstruction.

In emergency situations, hospitals do not always follow a DNR order. You need to tell everyone about the patient's wishes and have copies available to dispense as needed.

Even if a DNR is on the record, it is not automatic in many cases and in many facilities. As holder of a valid Power of Attorney, you must be prepared to discuss these options with the doctors.

If you opt to disconnect the patient from any life support, consider whether he should be an organ donor. With organ donation and organs compatible with possible recipients, his memory can be kept alive in up to a dozen ways and help many families.

Final Support

The biggest fear of many patients is the thought that they might die alone. A patient at Sacred Heart Medical Center in Eugene, Oregon, was near death and asked a nurse to stay with him. By the time she finished her rounds, he had already died. As a result of that experience, the nurse, Sandra Clarke, established a "No One Dies Alone" program. This volunteer program was designed so that someone will be available at all times to sit with a dying patient. Most of the programs are local in nature and have been started by various hospitals around the country. Nurse Clarke has written a book for those who would like to start a local organization.[31] Your local hospital or facility can get help in establishing a similar program by calling the Sacred Heart Medical Center program coordinator, Carleen McCornack at 541-335-2512 (CMcCornack@ peacehealth.org). This program is sponsored by Mission Services - PeaceHealth Oregon Region. The information contained in Clarke's operations manual includes steps to get started, how to recruit and keep volunteers, assessment information, and a variety of other forms and requirements. There are also similar programs sponsored by Veterans' groups. *No One Dies Alone* is a volunteer program and requires no nursing skills. The volunteer acts only as a companion, holding a hand, reading to the patient, playing music, or fluffing pillows.

This is one of many opportunities for support groups you should consider, especially if you are dealing with the end stages of life.

---

[31] No One Dies Alone Operations Manual by Susan Keane Baker is available. Contact www.peacehealth.org/oregon/ and search for *No One Dies Alone.*

Section IV - After Death

Death is always a shock, even when expected. When not expected, it is even worse. Shock, disbelief, hurt and confusion accompany grief. Search hard enough and you can find something to feel guilty about.

An Illustration

Quinn was helping a family move. A licensed tradesman by profession, he had knowledge of many things, including how to pack a truck, how to lift things, and how to put things together. The family offered to call a professional moving company but Quinn would not listen. He said that he had some skills in this area and wanted to help out of friendship. The move went smoothly and Quinn even returned the rented truck before going home for the night. The next morning, the family received a call from Quinn's employer. He was walking across a warehouse floor and collapsed. Within hours, the family was told that he had died immediately of a massive heart attack. The family expressed concern that they had been the cause of the attack, but learned later that Quinn came from a family with a long history of heart problems and he had complained earlier in the week of some chest pain, but did not investigate.

Don't blame yourself for tragedies. All you can do is the best you can.

All of the bad feelings are normal. If you did the best you could, that is all anyone can expect. The most common thought when someone in your care dies is, "What if I had only...?" The fact is, if you had only ... anything, it would have likely had little or no effect. Console yourself with the thought that you did everything you could and exercised your best judgment. Don't worry about what you might have done better, or what you might have done incorrectly. Especially when caring for the elderly, you need to accept death as the unavoidable finality of your efforts. Feel good about having done as much as possible for the patient when it counted, while she was alive. Remember her for the good times and her good deeds.

Some people can't remember anything about the death, while others want to know every detail. Some need to talk excessively while others can't speak at all. There is no such thing as a "normal" reaction. Every person reacts differently. You may want to see the formal notice in the local newspaper, touch the body, feel the patient's jewelry or a favorite item, or visit her favorite locations. Take the time to grieve in whatever way you feel is appropriate, without regard to what others may say or do. Choose to see yourself as one who has done the best job possible.

Arrangements

If the patient resided in a facility, the facility will notify the doctor who will, in turn, sign the death certificate. You may need to provide some information for that document. The death certificate will typically include date and place of birth, parents' names, residence, occupation (most recent occupation or Industry, not 'retired').

Also part of the form is information on disposition. That may be burial, cremation, donation, or mausoleum.

You will need to notify the funeral home. Use only reputable providers, who can help with the details and all the arrangements. If you do not already have a funeral home, the state should have a list of approved and experienced funeral directors. The funeral director needs to make the necessary arrangements and determine the funeral schedule with you. They will also place the proper advertisement in the local newspaper and work with you for any accompanying story. The funeral director should have a form which will help guide you in the proper information for the announcement, including your choice for memorial donations. A sample of one such form is located in Appendix E (beginning on page 176). Hopefully, most of these arrangements have been made ahead of time.

Once you have determined the details, you need to call family and friends. Set in motion a phone tree. Don't try to do everything yourself. If you have a job, remember to notify your boss, employees and/or co-workers.

If you are the cosigner on a safe deposit box, empty it immediately, before notifying the bank. After a death, the bank may freeze access to the box.

Later, you will need to notify any life insurance companies (with copies of the death certificate); health insurance company; any other insurance companies which may carry your loved one on the books (auto insurance, for example); a landlord, if applicable; and Social Security. If he is collecting Social Security, you may need to return the last check.

When you need a copy (one or more) of the death certificate, and if you don't know where to find one, contact the Centers for Disease Control and Prevention (CDC). This government agency maintains a directory of links to both state and foreign offices which are responsible for vital records, including death certificates. The links also explain the procedures and costs of obtaining those records.[32]

After everything has settled down, notify the monument company so they can arrange to put the date of death on the monument (if prepaid) or so you can make an appointment to select a monument.

Don't forget to cancel all the credit cards which may have been issued in your loved one's name.

It is difficult to accomplish these tasks when you are in the middle of grieving, but time is important.

Sometimes, items that can wait include the settling of any estate, including bequests to family and friends.

Bereavement

Bereavement fares are available from many airlines. In some cases, they involve modest

---

[32] www.cdc.gov/nchs/howto/w2w/w2welcom.htm. click on the state where the death occurred.

discounts. In other cases, the airlines may offer special rates. Some of the other airline rules may also not apply. Some carriers will allow for changes in plans without a surcharge. Others may make sure you get a seat, even if the flight is overbooked. These fares are available to relatives only. The airlines define a relative as loosely as possible. Typical of the definition is Delta Airlines' list, which includes everything from spouse or domestic partner to aunts, nieces and nephews, and even includes step-relationships and in-law relationships.

Your Medications

Part of the grieving process involves personal feelings. Some people are more vulnerable at what is a trying time. If you are on medications already, discuss your loss with your doctor. She may adjust the dosage for such things as antidepressants, tranquilizers or other medications for anxiety or sleeplessness. Some other items, such as blood pressure or sugar levels may need to be checked more often if you have problems in these areas. Don't try to adjust dosages or take anything else by yourself. Asking questions or taking precautions is **never** a bad thing. Keep to your normal routine (sleeping, eating) as much as possible.

Support Groups

Talking about your loved one is generally beneficial. Most of the time, friends and relatives tend to disappear shortly after the funeral. Consider a support group. Start with the hospital social service department. If that fails, contact mental health agencies in your city or ask your clergyperson. Select a support group which matches your current status. If you are newly bereaved, don't pick a group in which the losses are a year old. If your children are accompanying you, be sure the group has some age-appropriate members. If you are concerned about confidentiality, select a group which is not in your immediate area.

As an alternative, you can schedule one or more visits with a professional counselor, clergyperson or psychologist. Check with your insurance company to determine any coverage.

The Medical Community

Remember to write a note to each of the professionals who helped during the last days. The nurses and doctors who receive these notes appreciate the thoughtfulness which goes into them. By the same token, a true professional who cares for his patients will also send you a note of condolence. That is a sign of respect from a truly caring individual.

Discharge Summary

After the busy time immediately following a death, you should ask the facility for a discharge summary. That summary contains the nurses' notes as well as the physician's, and should indicate the care received, medications and other end-of-life information. This summary may be useful later when it may become important to know medical information to allow doctors to better treat another family member. Sometimes, the summary may lead to questions or other concerns about the death. Don't be afraid to ask those questions so that you know all the details.

When a patient dies, it is often a normal feeling that poor medical care or some error led to the death. On occasion, that is true. However, especially in the case of elderly patients, the desire to file a malpractice case should be tempered with reality. Since the elderly person may have little or no income and no future earning potential, the likelihood of a large award is minimal. Most malpractice awards are based, at least in part, on the lost income potential of the deceased.

Most attorneys will not take a case on contingency[33] and will require a sizeable advance retainer. Add that high expense to the time it usually takes for such a case to make its way through the court system and it is often not worth it. Sometimes, family members want to pursue the option of a suit to prevent the perceived error from happening again to someone else.

However, there may be better ways to accomplish that goal. Certainly consult with an attorney, especially one who specializes in sudden death or malpractice cases. There are some attorneys who specialize further in nursing home laws. Also, discuss your concerns with the state Ombudsman or licensing board.

Don't allow your feeling of loss to cloud your judgment about what may or may not be a case which ought to be pursued.

Those Left Behind

When an elderly person passes away, their elderly friends need support for their own grieving process. They may call you to reminisce, discuss their own problems, or just need to talk.

While these calls may seem bothersome, remember that they could be friends of 30, 40, or even more years who supported and comforted your loved one. They may have good memories to share. Those stories can bring you comfort and peace, as well as serving as a comforting gesture for them.

---

[33] Contingency cases involve no advance payments. The attorney takes a percentage plus expenses from any award.

Often, callers are lonely and want to recount how much their lives revolved around the deceased.

People will often make comments which are crude, if not cruel. "He's better off," or "Now you can get on with ...," are fairly common. Most of these comments are made because people often don't know what to say. The most appropriate comment is a simple, "I'm sorry." Assume that the visitor is sincere in his condolences but unsure about what to say.

You do not need to answer any question or comment which is inappropriate or concerns something you don't wish to discuss. Gently tell such a person that you would rather not discuss that topic.

Have patience. Be kind. Think of the meaning of those relationships and recognize that their grief needs to be acknowledged and honored. Consider the calls tributes to a special person.

Questions Answered

Even when death is expected, it is a difficult time for all members of the family, especially for the person who has spent so much time providing care. You have the right to have all your questions answered by the physicians or other professionals, even after time has passed. Most people cannot remember the questions while sitting at a death bed. After death, the rush of activity may push your concerns to the back burner. Later, you may find some lingering issues or worries. As the caregiver, schedule a visit with the doctor or another medical, psychological, or religious professional. Review the areas of concern until you are satisfied that the care was appropriate.

If those meetings seem to indicate one or more errors, consult with an independent evaluator, such as another doctor or even an attorney. Remember, if you have a power of attorney, you may be able to obtain the complete medical record for this review. A Power of Attorney ends at death, but most facilities will still honor some of your requests. Otherwise, you may need to also be the executor of the deceased's estate. Generally, these meetings can help you and your family to resolve any anxieties.

These actions should help you in the grieving process.

Autopsy

An autopsy is an examination of a body to determine cause of death or other conditions.

An autopsy is generally ordered in the case of someone dying alone, unexpectedly, or suspiciously. In those cases, you will have no choice in the matter. Legal reasons for an autopsy will override religious considerations. An insurance company may also ask for an autopsy if they feel the cause of a sudden death is questionable.

Other reasons for an autopsy may include teaching, research, or the discovery of contributory causes of death.

An Illustration

Teresa died at 25. She had complained of a headache, collapsed and died. Teresa had a long history of drug abuse, but had been in a rehabilitation program. The initial cause of death was listed as an aneurism. The doctors were unclear about whether she had started using drugs again or whether there were other underlying causes. The doctors insisted upon performing an autopsy. During the autopsy, it was determined that Teresa took a headache medication for a second time earlier than she should have. They indicated that this appar-

ent overdose contributed to her death as a secondary cause.

In cases where there is any question, the doctors may perform an autopsy without permission or consultation.

If you have any questions which might be answered by an autopsy, you can also ask for one. Don't ask for an autopsy unless there is a specific reason to have one.

If you are considering an autopsy be sure the person performing the autopsy is licensed and qualified. Check on the costs associated with the procedure, including the transportation. Read carefully any documents associated with the autopsy.

Costs associated with an autopsy ordered by the state are the responsibility of the state. If you request an autopsy, the costs are your responsibility. If the autopsy in not performed when the patient dies, there may be transportation costs in addition to the costs for the procedure itself.

If you ask for an autopsy, you should ask where the report will be sent and if you will receive a copy. You should also know how long the procedure will take so you can make whatever funeral arrangements need to be made.

You should also be aware of the possibility that, if the autopsy discovers anything unusual, the doctor may be required to notify local authorities. Also, an insurance company may refuse to pay a claim under some circumstances. Your autopsy may prompt the insurance company to investigate further.

Some disorders which may be discovered during an autopsy may lead to further investigation of family members for inherited conditions.

Waiting for the results and conclusions of an autopsy can place added stress on you and the family. Unnecessary procedures and tests do not generally help anyone. If not required by the state, keep in mind that some religions do not allow for autopsies.

An Illustration

Raisa had suffered four miscarriages. One of the doctors indicated that the problem might be because of a genetic predisposition. Raisa went to a specialist who determined that she had a defect in a gene which would prevent her from carrying a fetus to term. The doctor suggested that the problem may be inherited and that testing on Raisa's 84-year-old mother could prove conclusively the history of the problem. As an only child and with an elderly mother, Raisa declined the test because she felt there was nothing to be gained.

Don't allow any procedure which does not accomplish anything.

Children's Reactions

Children react to death in different ways. They may take several months or years beyond the event to comprehend fully the events surrounding a death. Some react with tears. Others seem oblivious.

Don't get upset if a child asks the same questions over and over. Let the child experience the grief at her own pace. Reassure her that she is all right and that you are prepared to listen if she wants to talk. Don't press her to talk. She will discuss the issues when she is ready. She may not want to talk about her loss because she does not want to upset the family.

You should carefully monitor how the child is coping with the death and consult, if necessary, with the pediatrician, school counselor or psychologist. Recognize that a child may only partially understand what has happened and can easily misinterpret what she hears from adults and friends.

When a child does ask questions, don't provide long details and explanations. Answer the question you are asked without embellishing and in terms appropriate to the child's age. Let the child take the lead. She will ask more questions or more detailed questions when she is ready.

Don't force a child to go to the cemetery. Age is not the determining factor. Some younger children want to go, while some older children cannot face that prospect.

Adult Reactions

Men and women react to a loss differently. In one survey (not a formal, statistically significant one), men were seen to move on faster and tended to look ahead. They look for something new, such as a hobby, sports, travel, or social activities. They tend to begin dating more quickly, even during the grieving process. Men are generally used to being cared for and seem to need the caregiving almost immediately. Men may see change as beneficial.

Men who relied on others for housekeeping, finances, or shopping may appear helpless in those areas. They may search for an easy and quick fix even while still experiencing grief and loss.

Women, on the other hand, generally want to spend time with friends, children, grandchildren or support groups. They may attend their house of worship more regularly than they had in the past. They want to take the time to think about the memories their loved one generated.

Both men and women undergo a transformation when a spouse dies. One who made few decisions might need to become more extroverted and to find ways to handle decision making. Some feel they only need to please themselves without concern for others. No course of action is incorrect. Don't criticize someone who pursues a course different from one you might dictate. Each person handles grief in a different way.

While many feel that they made a promise to a dying spouse not to remarry, that is not necessarily the best course. After an appropriate time of mourning, it is reasonable to encourage the survivor to re-enter the social circles which exist. Men and women who remarry often select a new partner who has similar characteristics to their previous spouse. You should understand that this action is normal. For that very reason, there is a possibility that the new relationship may not prove fruitful.

Employment Concerns

You may be forced back to work earlier than you would like, by work-related activities, economic concerns, or even a boss who is unwilling to extend your time away.

People react differently. You may be anxious to return to work. You may want some more time off to mourn. Monitor yourself. You have suffered a major life crisis. Don't try to pretend it doesn't exist. Recognize that it will take time to get back into your normal life.

When you return, your co-workers and others may offer condolences or offer to help. Some may probe for details. Take their concern as the caring interest of your peers. Thank them and move on. You don't need to provide any details you don't feel comfortable with. Many people don't know what to say. Some will ask inappropriate questions. Others will merely say "I'm sorry." Still others may say nothing, fearing that any comment will not be well received.

Some well-meaning people will even try to be helpful by suggesting financial changes, such as moving to a less expensive home, especially if you lost a spouse. Don't make any sudden decisions. You should take the time to consult with everyone you trust, from the clergy to a financial planner, accountant, or attorney. Take the time to be sure that any decision (including doing nothing) is the correct decision for you.

Vacation

After the major trauma of a death, there are responsibilities that follow: funeral arrangements, finances, estate issues, insurance details, credit card cancellations, and acknowledgements. The added work can be exhausting, both physically and mentally. Those who go through this kind of trauma generally do not realize the habits that change; eating, drinking and sleeping.

The amount of written work increases. The number of telephone calls increases. The necessary responses increase. As a caregiver, the sudden change from caring for a person to caring for things is abrupt and often disconcerting. There is a period of adjustment that must be endured while grieving.

You can benefit from a change of scene, rest, and relaxation. You may need some time alone to think, plan, review past decisions, or just sleep. While most of us choose to vacation with others, being alone can help you become rejuvenated. Being waited on, pampered and out of the hubbub of daily living can be refreshing.

An Illustration

Sally acted as caregiver for her mother for several years. After lingering first in Sally's house, and then in a nursing home, her mother finally passed away. Sally thought about the many years they had enjoyed going to the beach. She made plans to spend several days at a beach far from where she had grown up and where no one knew her. Sally returned well rested and ready to dive into her everyday responsibilities.

A few days away can help you move on with life.

Sometimes having no demands and nothing on your schedule will provide the break you need. Take a friend or significant other if that is your choice. Pick an activity different from your normal routine. Take a foliage trip, a day cruise, see a play, go on a retreat, or just go sightseeing. What you do is immaterial, as long as you do something.

An Illustration

Oscar emigrated to the United States with his wife. They left their entire family behind. Shortly after their arrival, Oscar had a heart attack and died. His wife had no other relatives in this country, had made few friends, and was not helped by the support group she attended. Finally, she realized that she was not doing well and decided to visit friends and relatives in Europe. Her cries of grief were mixed with tears of joy at seeing and meeting with old friends and seeing old places. She did well after that trip.

Sometimes, a change of scenery is indicated.

Grief Support Groups

If you have decided to try a support group, contact the local hospital and the other agencies we have mentioned to find an appropriate choice. To help decide which support group is appropriate for you, consider the following questions:

What am I hoping to gain? Am I looking for a way to vent, a place to cry, to obtain advice, or comfort?

Will I find information? Will the support group offer advice or just be a place for me to listen to others and for them to listen to me? Is there literature or web site information being given out?

Are there guest speakers? Am I looking for information which can be supplied by grief counselors or other professionals?

Can I bring someone with me? Sometimes, it is comforting to have a friend who will provide support just by being there.

Is there a cost? You need to determine if the cost is moderate or beyond your means. You should also check to see if any cost is covered by your insurance mental health benefits.

Is the group confidential? Some people want absolute confidentiality about what is said in a support group meeting. Others may not care.

Do I have to speak? If you want to share your feelings, that will not be a problem. If you would rather sit quietly, that should be allowed also, and without your needing to talk until you are ready.

Are there any rules within the group? You should know how detailed you should be about your experiences.

Who sponsors the group? If it is hospital based, does the hospital supply a moderator or professional to help with the grieving process?

Where in the grieving process are the other members? Only you can know what you want from a group. Having people in various stages of grief may be good or it may be bad. Sometimes, those who have been in the group for a longer period of time can help you more than those who are in the same stage of loss.

Is there any follow up? After the sessions are complete, does anyone call to see if you are all right?

Will one-on-one counseling be offered? Is there a counselor who can listen at the sessions and meet with you afterward or at another time, if you would like such a meeting?

Sleep

Grief often affects sleep. It is important to maintain a proper sleep schedule. Daytime naps can interfere with your usual pattern. Moreover, grieving may cause disruptions in sleep, bad dreams, or feelings of anxiety or chaos upon waking. The hectic pace of clearing the paperwork tied to the death can disrupt your ability to fall asleep or stay asleep as well.

If the symptoms do not lessen over time, consult with your doctor. Some of the stress can be reduced through medication, reading scriptures, writing in a diary, or taking care of pets.

Don't try to do everything yourself. Set a reasonable pace and allow others to help whenever necessary. Sometimes simple pleasures can have a helpful effect.

Keep a sleep log to follow the course of your improvement.

Accept the Loss

Even when they don't recognize it, many people try to hide their grief. Signs may include saying, "I'll get over it," or "He had it much worse than I did," may be a cover to avoid confronting the grief and learning to work through it. You must give yourself permission to grieve and continue with your own life. By accepting those kinds of statements, well-meaning friends and family may be interfering with the recovery process. Only when someone points out that you are denying or hiding your grief can you realize the turmoil caused by those denials.

You might hide your own grief in hopes of supporting another or denying your true feelings.

Instead, surround yourself with support systems and supportive people. In many cases, your clergyperson can help.

Settling the Estate

Don't be in a hurry to settle the estate. This procedure can often take a year or longer. This time is still a period of grieving and collecting the necessary records.

Bills

Bills and other debts begin to show up after a death. You need to know your responsibilities and rights. You may need to consult with an attorney. Don't rush to pay bills. You are under no obligation to pay the debts incurred by the deceased. You can call any debtor and explain that the responsible party has died, and that any payments which may be forthcoming must wait for the estate to be settled. If the remainder of the estate is large enough to cover every bill, you might pay them in full. Once you have notified a debtor, that debtor should not be contacting you any further. Keep a journal of who you talk to and any other details you can. Better still, notify the debtors in writing, keeping copies. You, as an individual, are not responsible for any of the deceased's bills unless you incurred them.

If the estate does not cover every debt, **be careful**. If you pay any single bill, other debtors may go to court to claim favoritism. More importantly, a debtor may claim that, because you paid a bill or part of a bill, that you have affirmed the bill as your own. You might then be held responsible not only for that bill, but for all unpaid bills of the deceased.

Some collectors will ask you to pay just a small portion of a bill to show "good faith" or so they can show their boss that they are doing their job. **Don't**. That small payment reaffirms the bill and the collector will then insist that the bill is yours. That action also re-dates the statute of limitations and starts the clock over again so you can be subject to harassment longer.

Finally, recognize that there are scam artists everywhere. Some even read the obituary notices and prey on the grieving. They may be selling something or trying to collect for a supposed order placed by the deceased but not yet delivered. On the day of the funeral or service, have someone "housesit" so that no robberies or other mishaps occur, especially if notices have appeared in newspapers.

Final record keeping

Put all of the patient's paperwork in a safe place and keep it for at least several years. The statutes of limitations for various items range from one year to seven years. If you still have credit cards in the deceased's name, cut them up and don't use them. Their use could bring up other problems. Any valuable items should be insured under your homeowners' or tenants' policy or the policy of those who have them. Remember to get updated appraisals, especially for jewelry items which may be worth more as antiques than gems.

Section V - Questions and Answers

All of the topics covered here have also been addressed in the earlier parts of the book. Each point covered will either answer a question or address a concern. While we may refer in a question to a mother or brother, the answers are meant to be general examples and apply to people in various situations.

Financial

Q. How do I know if my parent is capable of making medical or financial decisions?

A. Ask yourself if earlier decisions are
    consistent with her present statements.
    Is she refusing medications she once
    took without question and which appear
    to work properly? You may also need to
    consult with your parent's physicians,
    social workers, attorney or accountant.
    Sometimes, even neighbors may reveal
    issues needing examination.

Q. **My father is collecting social security
    disability but is overwhelmed by the
    paperwork required for re-evaluations
    and re-certifications.**

A. Consult with your local Social Security
    office. You can help complete the forms.
    You need to have a Power of Attorney
    for medical reasons. There is a place on
    the forms for you to indicate that you
    are acting on behalf of the patient. You
    may need to send a copy of your Power
    of Attorney with the forms. Do not send
    the original. You may also find or
    request an advocate to act as scribe.

Q. **My parents own a home near mine.
    They can no longer afford the upkeep
    and still provide for living costs, in-
    cluding medications and food.**

A. If the house is paid off, one of the
    possibilities is a reverse mortgage,
    where a fixed amount is given to them
    each month. That amount plus interest
    is repaid when the property is sold.
    Consult with their attorney to see if this
    plan is appropriate for them.

Q. **I am caregiver for my elderly parent.
    My siblings leave all the care to me.
    Although they send money, they
    offer no other support for me or my**

family. How can I involve them in the care and decisions?

A. Make regular family conference calls and notes with updates. You can also use e-mail blasts, which are becoming more popular. Ask their opinions and involve them in decisions. In addition, you may look to other agencies for support.

Q. **My sibling has a Power of Attorney for my parent, but she seems to be making poor decisions. How should I proceed?**

A. Consult with all parties involved to seek amicable and appropriate solutions. If necessary, consult with an attorney.

Q. **My mother refuses to make a will and the family is concerned that assets will be lost.**

A. First, you need to explain that a will does not mean she is ready to die. It only means she is helping to assure that there will be no out-of-control arguments. Second, assets are not lost, but if the family begins to fight over them, much of the estate can be eaten up in legal fees. Finally, explain to your loved one that the arguments which can occur over assets can lead to a permanent rift in families and their relationships. Explain probate, including the delays and headaches which result from dying intestate (with no will). If necessary, ask a trusted attorney for guidance.

Q. **My mother left her money and other assets to a favorite charity. In the years before her death, she constantly borrowed money from the**

family without repayment, and owes many family members money. Should we challenge the will?

A. Consult with an attorney. Depending upon the size of the estate, it may cost you more than you can recover.

Q. **If relatives argue about the division of property, what can be done?**

A. First, search for a Last Will and Testament. The executor of the will should be able to solve any arguments. If there is no will, try to recall the wishes of the deceased and attempt to follow those wishes. If that is not possible, it is preferable to try sharing equitably rather than using the services of an attorney or the courts. The general result of a court fight is that the estate disappears in legal fees. In the case of jewelry, you may want to have updated appraisals so that the sharing will be fair.

Q. **My mother refuses to see a dentist, claiming lack of funds.**

A. When your mother even refuses to let you pay the cost, consider the low or no cost clinics in your area, generally affiliated with dental schools. Take the focus off the difficulties by offering to drive back and forth and include lunch.

Q. **My elderly mother refuses to discuss her future. She has given the family no information about her health, finances or banking, nor will she share her final wishes. Can she be forced to share this vital information?**

A. You should check with her attorney and question other family members who may be able to shed some light on the situation. Also, consult with her physician to be sure she IS capable.

Living arrangements

Q. My mother insists on living alone. We are afraid of what may happen.

A. First try to reason with her and explain that you will try to be sure that her freedom is not taken away. Also enlist the aid of her doctors. Often, a doctor may be able to convince an elderly patient that it is time to give up some freedom in return for safety. Some people require a home assessment by local agencies.

Q. I am planning to have my elderly grandmother move in with my family. She is not able to care for herself. Where can I find information and training about caregiving?

A. Some elder service organizations, both state and local, supply free training. Talk to the physician for a nursing assessment that will have safety accommodations made in the home. Home-bound patients may also be entitled to at-home care. Social workers may also be helpful. The physician should have access to the needed resources.

Medication Issues

Q. My mother is not following the instructions on her medication containers.

A. Take notes about what she is actually doing compared to what the medication calls for. Speak with the pharmacist and the doctor as soon as possible for guidance.

Q. I don't think my brother is taking his medications correctly.

A. Check the instructions on the pill bottles. Check the count, ask for written instructions from the physician or the pharmacist. There are pill counter devices and other aids to help keep track of medications. Some can hold a week's worth of pills for four-times-a-day administration.

Q. The emergency room physicians seem to overload my father with medications. He is getting confused. What is my next step?

A. It is critical to follow up with a primary physician. Emergency room physicians are good for emergencies. Try to encourage regular check-ups with your father's primary care physician. Share your concerns with the doctor.

Q. My sick husband claims that the multiple medications he was ordered to take are making him sleepy and sick. He is refusing to take them. The doctor insists that he take them. I am concerned.

A. Talk to the pharmacist and, if indicated, do not hesitate to get a second opinion. Inform your husband's physician if your husband is resistant.

Q. My father is very ill and requires medication. However, I suspect that

the multiple medications are creating problems.

A. Compile a complete list of every medication, both prescription and over-the-counter. Include doses and frequency. Discuss the entire list with the doctor and your pharmacist. Relate your concerns and ask about any possible interactions and side effects. Include in this assessment any homeopathic remedies he may be taking.

Q. **A specialist prescribed a strong medication for depression. It has led to side effects which the doctor said would go away with time. They have not but the doctor remains aloof. What should I do?**

A. Consult with the primary care doctor. Ask what steps should be followed next. If you do not receive appropriate answers, seek a second opinion.

Medical and Mental Concerns

Q. **My father does not seem to understand what the doctor is telling him.**

A. Go with your father to the medical appointment and tell the doctor your perception of the situation.

Q. **The doctor does not fully explain things to my mother and always appears rushed.**

A. Make a late-in-the-day appointment so you don't disrupt the doctor's busy routine. Take the time to make your concerns clear and insist that the explanations be more complete, perhaps in writing.

Q. My brother's doctor is always busy. I don't think my brother is getting answers to all his questions during his appointments.

A. Go to the next appointment and, while in the doctor's office, ask your brother if he has any questions. Prepare a list of your concerns in advance. Present them to the doctor.

Q. I am the only living relative for my elderly aunt. I don't know anything about her medical history, although I think she has been neglecting her health. Where do I begin?

A. Inquire about a Power of Attorney and a Living Will. Discuss these with your relative and an attorney. Other professionals may be able to elicit answers.

Q. My husband's friend died recently. Since that time, he has become irritable and explosive. I think he may be depressed and worried about his own mortality. What should I do?

A. Listen to what he says. Try to join a support group, or both. Tell your husband's doctor. Insist that he have a check up to be sure there is no medical issue. You can also make an appointment with a therapist.

Q. My grandmother is giving away all her possessions, even though she is not ill or dying. Family members are angry and many want those items, even pictures. Should she be stopped?

A. She may be depressed or suffering from dementia. Notify her physician immediately.

Distance

Q. My parents live in another state. I am concerned about their failing health and their safety. What can I do from a distance?

A. Contact the elder service department in your town and in the town where your parents live, for more information. Share your concerns with physicians. Have a neighbor phone or check in with your parents. Consider hiring a private therapist (physical therapist or occupational therapist) to inspect the premises and make recommendations.

Q. I have been caregiver for my parents. They now wish to sell their home and move to a warmer climate. How can I insure their safety and appropriate medical care from a distance?

A. First, talk to their physicians for recommendations in the new setting. Locate a good Realtor. Call to gather information about senior services from the town they are considering. Collect brochures and other written materials.

Memory Issues

Q. My parent has become forgetful and I am concerned that her physician does not seem to notice.

A. Your parent may need referrals to appropriate specialists. Share your feelings with the doctor. Give specific examples. Keep a log. Include how frequently these episodes occur.

Q. I need to repeat everything I tell my father. He forgets what I said almost immediately. What can I do?

A. Keep language to a minimum. Give him information in short bursts and have your father repeat the information back to you. Also, inform the doctor. It could be hearing, dementia or other medical conditions. Use face to-face contact as well as eye contact.

Visiting

Q. Ever since my mother received the prognosis of irreversible ailments, she has curtailed all activities, including meeting with friends or going out.

A. This behavior may be a sign of depression. She may require medication or other therapy designed to help her cope with this major life crisis.

Q. My husband has been told by his doctor that he has only a few years to live, because of a combination of ailments. Since that time, my husband refuses to go out, meet with friends or participate in the activities which we always shared. What should I do?

A. Bring friends and visitors to the house, if possible. Have the physician evaluate his mental status.

Q. Should visitors be encouraged for someone who is terminally ill?

A. Yes, most of the time. Consult with the staff of the nursing home or hospital or consult with the doctor. Some people may require that visits be short or restricted on some days. Some visitors may also benefit from a meeting with a social worker or other professional prior to or following the visit. Everyone must be prepared and should be counseled ahead of time if there is anything unusual they should expect.

Q. I am becoming anxious because my father has started to make inappropriate comments to my young children during visits. When I remind him to monitor his speech, he seems unconcerned. How should I handle this?

A. Keep visits short. Explain the illness, which is possibly dementia, to children. Refocus the patient onto other topics.

Q. My elderly mother visits her dying friend in the hospital. After every visit, my mother is upset for days. Should I intervene?

A. Try to go with your mother and plan lunch, shopping and support by just listening to her. She is grieving in advance. She can also join a support group or see an individual therapist if needed.

Q. A neighbor of my mother constantly visits and keeps asking for her possessions. How should we stop this behavior?

A. Try to have someone present during these visits. Put possessions out of sight or locked up as much as possible. Assess whether your mother is being unduly influenced and is mentally well.

Injuries

Q. **Every time I visit my mother, I notice bruises. She laughs and claims she falls down. I think my father, who is suffering from dementia and living at home, may be abusing her. What should I do?**

A. Contact the physicians for both parents and report your observations. There are assessments that can be done in the home to evaluate the problem.

Daily Living

Q. **What should I do if my father loses the desire to eat or drink?**

A. Contact the physician immediately. Options may include changes in medication, the services of a nutritionist, or medical or psychological evaluations. Sometimes, gentle encouragement may work. Suggest small meals or healthy snacks. Finally consider nutrition drinks which can substitute for full meals.

Q. **My co-workers do not understand the stress I am experiencing because of the responsibilities I have taking care of my sick family member.**

A. Don't talk about it at work. Limit conversations to after-hours. Co-workers may not want to be distracted. Join a support group or see a therapist. As a last resort, consider some time off under the Family Medical Leave Act.

Q. How do I get handicapped registration plates? Can I get them for my car when my father is not the owner?

A. Contact your state Motor Vehicle department. Most will have a form which must be completed and signed by both you and the doctor. You can get either plates or a placard but you are only allowed to take advantage of them when your father is in the car.

Q. My mother uses a wheelchair. I take her to shopping malls and other facilities. I am concerned about safety, for her, for me and for others because of hazards in the roadway and walkway. What should I do?

A. Consult with a physical or occupational therapist for instructions and assistance. Contact the Public Works department of the city to discuss accessibility to various locations.

Q. My elderly mother insists that she is capable of driving, even though I can see that her reflexes and reactions have slowed. I am worried about her getting into an accident.

A. First, contact your mother's physician or the Motor Vehicle department to discuss options. They may include an elderly drivers' refresher course, another road test, or other forms of transportation for elderly or disabled people. If you are concerned, take away the keys. It is better to have your mother mad at you than to have her seriously injured in an accident. Also, check on "The Ride," door-to-door bus service for the elderly or disabled. This service may go by a different name in your area. Consult with an attorney as needed.

Nursing Home

Q. My mother made me promise never to put her in a nursing home, but the doctor insists that she needs one because she now requires 24-hour care. How should I deal with this?

A. Speak to the physician for advice and, if possible, have her visit her future placement. The nursing staff as well as the social workers may be helpful.

Q. My parents are fast reaching the point where they will need a nursing home. They have no assets and do not own a home. I have limited finances. Who is going to pay for their care? What are my options?

A. Contact elder service agencies in your area as well as the Social Security office. Research Medicare and Medicaid for further options and information.

Q. My mother is in a distant nursing home. I don't think she is receiving appropriate care. There are no beds available in nearby homes. What can I do?

A. Address your concerns in writing with the chief administrator. If that does not resolve your concerns, contact the ombudsman in your state (every state has one). Also speak with the physician and make him aware of your concerns.

Q. My grandmother constantly complains about pain. The nursing home

staff does not seem to be able to control it. What should I do?

A. Some facilities have physicians on staff or on call who specialize and are trained in pain management. Ask the home to arrange for a consultation. If you need more help, contact the Hospice agency in your area.

Q. I am caregiver to a diabetic in a nursing home. She constantly sneaks candy and other inappropriate food, causing medical problems. The staff does not seem to be able to control the behavior. Do I have options?

A. Contact the chief administrator. The patient needs to have her room and belongings checked several times each day. Check to be sure she is not truly hungry and that her dietary needs are being met. Also make sure that portion sizes are appropriate. Ask if the candy fetish could be an early sign of dementia or other condition.

Q. The staff at the nursing home became annoyed when I insisted on remaining with my loved one and holding her hand. The nurse insisted that she was "holding on" just for me and I should leave the room. Should she have intervened?

A. The real question is "what is in the best interest of the patient?" Ask the physician for guidance. Don't blame the nurse too much. Even when seemingly insensitive, the nurse is trying to do the best job she can.

Final Plans

Q. My grandmother wants to be dressed in her wedding gown for her funeral. Some family members do not consider it appropriate and feel uneasy. Should her request be granted?

A. Unless there is a specific reason to deny the request, why not? Discuss the request with the funeral director. Also ask her physician if the request is a sign of dementia.

Q. My granddaughter has a terminal illness. She wants her school to plan an elaborate service for her young classmates. Is this wise?

A. Explain to your granddaughter that you will discuss it with the school. Schools generally have rules about such services. Reassure your granddaughter that you will try to investigate.

Q. My sister lives in a small home. When her husband dies, is it appropriate to use my house for memorial visits instead of hers?

A. Absolutely. The main purpose for memorial visits is to offer support and comfort during a trying time. The location is not important.

Q. My father is a veteran. Are there people I need to contact when he dies?

A. Contact the Veteran's Agent in your town. The agent can also help coordinate Veterans' benefits.

Q. People constantly break into funeral processions. Can this be avoided?

A. The funeral director needs to be vigilant and should consider a police escort if necessary and appropriate. One way to minimize these intrusions is to ask the funeral director to have the procession move slowly. Therefore, cars will be closer together and there won't be space for cutting in.

Q. **Does a funeral home have the right to insist that an insurance policy be signed over as future payment for burial?**

A. Not as a rule, but making the funeral home the beneficiary of such a policy is the normal method of prepaying for a funeral. We do not recommend that a prepayment be made without an insurance policy because you would then be restricted to that funeral home.

Q. **What should be done regarding children, funerals and other activities related to death and dying?**

A. Children should participate if they feel they can manage. Children should not be forced to participate and may need time to process a loss. Some children can tolerate and understand more than others. Consult with the pediatrician or therapist for guidance.

Q. **At a recent funeral, the young children of the deceased were sobbing hysterically. We could not even hear the clergyperson offer the eulogy. How should this be handled?**

A. The clergyperson may be able to assist the children then resume the pulpit. If there is unmanageable hysteria, the children should be removed and consoled in another location.

Q. What can be done if children seem uncooperative at a funeral?

A. It is important to determine the reasons for the behavior. Children do not always understand the customs, traditions, or procedures. It may be a child's first experience at a funeral. Some children are not mature enough to assume the needed responsibilities. A professional or a member of the clergy may be able to involve themselves and help families to address these issues.

Q. Family members felt moved by the words of one of the speakers at the funeral. Is it acceptable to ask for a copy of the eulogy?

A. Yes. However, it might be appropriate to ask the speakers in advance if they wish to give you a copy. That would be helpful to some family members and should not be considered rude by any speaker.

Q. The funeral director was very nice to the family throughout the ordeal. Is it acceptable to send him a gift to say "thank you?" What would be appropriate?

A. A brief letter of thanks would be appropriate. The funeral director may have a favorite charity and a donation in his name would be appreciated.

Q. How much should be written on the preprinted acknowledgement cards given out by the funeral home?

A. There is no rule. Some people find writing a brief note comforting. Others prefer to do very little. People appreciate receiving a handwritten comment. Don't forget, others are grieving also. It is more important to not have long delays in sending the cards.

Q. Why do I continue to receive mail for my deceased family member even though I notified the companies that she is no longer alive?

A. There is nothing more difficult than getting off a mailing list. Once you have notified a party, you have no further responsibility and you are not responsible for any charges which may be incurred because of improper activities. Do not open the mail. Write "Deceased, Return to Sender" on the envelope and drop it in the mail. Remember that you are not responsible for any items mailed to your address. Ignore any demands for payment because unordered items are legally considered gifts.

Q. Does the death of a person invalidate a Power-of-Attorney?

A. Yes. If you need to access medical or other records, be prepared to consult with an attorney to determine the protocol you need to follow. It is best to contact an attorney before you actually need one, so you can be prepared and have appropriate instructions. Sometimes, written, notarized instructions before death will go a long way to avoiding problems.

Q. How do I handle insurance policies after an accidental death?

A. Notify each insurance company that the patient has died. You will need to provide the policy number for each policy and a copy of the death certificate for each company. If the company insists on a notarized copy, you will need to get extra copies from the town. Payment should be made directly to the beneficiary listed on each policy. Check to see if there is an additional amount due because the death was accidental. If the insurance company shirks their responsibility to pay promptly, consult an attorney.

Q. An aunt requested a photo of my father after he died and was in a casket. Is it necessary or appropriate?

A. It is up to you, but for some people, it helps the grieving process. Ask the funeral director for guidance.

Q. I talk to my grandmother, even though she has been deceased for over a year. My friends and family urge me to seek professional help, even though I tell them I find it soothing. Am I crazy?

A. Absolutely not. This behavior can go on for years. As long as you are functioning daily in an appropriate manner, you are most likely working through the grieving process. Habits of a lifetime, such as talking to a grandmother, are hard to break.

Afterword

We hope we have made your path easier
and that we have taken away many of the fears
and concerns a caregiver normally has. Since
you have reached this point, you have
experienced the trials and tribulations, the ups
and downs, the good and the bad.

You will undoubtedly reflect on your
experiences in the days, months and even
years to come. Don't berate yourself; all you
can ever do is take heart that you cared, you
did, you loved, you worked, and most important, you made a difference.

Feel good that you made a difference in the
life and well-being of your loved one and
yourself.

An Illustration

*Ernesto spent several years helping his
wife through her final, lingering illness.
During that time, she was cared for first at
home, and finally through the local hospice
agency. After her death, Ernesto decided to*

continue his good works and volunteered with the local home health and hospice agency. He served in a variety of tasks several days each week.

Making a difference can be a rewarding experience even after the death of a loved one and even if you don't know the recipient.

Your task as caregiver may have ended, but life will go on. Good luck.

Appendix A - Emergency Response

These are some of the plans for emergency response. All offer either bracelets with a call button or necklaces with a call button. Research some of these and enroll in whichever plan you like. These plans are headquartered in the United States, have web sites you can access, and have toll-free phone numbers. There are similar plans available in other countries.[34] At the same time, check to see if the costs associated with these programs are either covered by insurance or if there are some area social service agencies which will help with the cost. We have tried to indicate some of the extra features offered by these providers. This is not meant to be a complete list and is

---

[34] These are not in any particular order and this is not meant to be a complete list.

accurate according to company web sites as of the publication date of this book.

- Philips Lifeline
  - www.LifeLineSystems.com
    800-380-3111
    - Medical and appointment reminders
    - Voice Clock
    - Hands free telephone answering
    - Speaker phone base unit
- LifeStation Medical Monitoring
  - www.LifeStation.com
    800-884-8888
    - 30-day money back trial
    - Automatic weekly test timer
    - Waterproof help button
- Connect America
  - www.MedicalAlarm.com
    800-800-1960
    - Waterproof help button
    - Inform emergency staff of medical conditions
- American Medical Alarms
  - www.AmericanMedicalAlarms.com
    800-542-0438
    - Water resistant help button
    - Backup batteries
    - Lockbox available to have a key nearby
- Medic Alert Foundation
  - www.MedicAlert.org
    888-633-4298
    - On-line health record
    - Health record bracelets
    - E-health key, medical records on computer memory stick
    - Self test daily
    - Automatically checks pendant battery daily
- Pioneer Emergency Bodyguard
  - www.PioneerEmergency.com
    800-274-8274

- Temperature sensors
- Battery backup
- Waterproof buttons

All of these companies offer 24 hour monitoring. It is your job to make sure the patient is always wearing the response button, even in the shower and when sleeping, if it is safe.

Appendix B -
Hearing and Vision

This list contains some of the organizations which serve and assist those who are either deaf or blind or have disabilities in those areas. Many of these have local chapters, but you can get guidance and referrals from the many national groups:[35]

- American Foundation for the Blind
  - www.afb.org
    800-232-5463
- Association of Blind Citizens
  - www.BlindCitizens.org
    781-961-1023
- National Family Association for Deaf-Blind
  - www.nfadb.org
    800-255-0411
- American Association for the Deaf-Blind

---

[35] Not meant to be a complete list.

- o www.aadb.org
  301-495-4403
- National Association of the Deaf
  - o www.nad.org
    301-587-1788
- Alexander Graham Bell Association for the Deaf and Hard of Hearing
  - o www.agbell.org
    202-337-5220
- New Eyes for the Needy
  - o www.neweyesfortheneedy.org
    973-376-4903

Appendix C - Animals

There are organizations which train animals to assist people with disabilities. The most well know animals are seeing eye dogs, but there are other uses. For more information about working animals, try:

- Guiding eyes for the Blind
    - www.GuidingEyes.org
      800-942-0149
- Keystone Human Services
    - www.KeystoneHumanService s.org
      888-377-6504
- The Seeing Eye, Inc.
    - www.SeeingEye.org
      973-539-4425
- Eye Dog Foundation for the Blind
    - www.EyeDogFoundation.org
      800-393-3641

Appendix D - Family and Medical Leave

The Family and Medical Leave Act (FMLA)[36] is Public Law 103-3 and was enacted on February 5, 1993.

Congress has found that:

- the number of single-parent households and two-parent households in which the single parent or both parents work is increasing significantly;
- the lack of employment policies to accommodate working parents can force

---

[36] This is not the complete law. We are reprinting only those portions which are important to this book and paraphrasing other portions

- individuals to choose between job security and parenting;
- there is inadequate job security for employees who have serious health conditions that prevent them from working for temporary periods;

The purpose of this act is:

- to balance the demands of the workplace with the needs of families;
- to entitle employees to take reasonable leave for medical reasons, for the birth or adoption of a child, and for the care of a child, spouse or parent who has a serious health condition;
- to minimize the potential for employment discrimination on the basis of sex by ensuring that leave is available for eligible medical reasons and for compelling family reasons, on a gender-neutral basis.

Employer definitions

The employer is any person or company who employs 50 or more employees for each day during 20 or more calendar weeks in the current or previous year. It also includes any person who acts in the interest of the employer or any successor (for instance, if the company is sold).

You are not included as an eligible employee if you are an officer or employee of the Federal government or if the company does not employ at least 50 workers. If the company has multiple locations, you are covered if there are 50 employees at worksites within 75 miles.

Requirements for Leave

An eligible employee is one who has been employed for at least 12 months by the employer from whom leave is desired; and

Has worked at least 1,250 hours for that employer during the previous 12 months.

Any leave granted under this position shall be unpaid, unless there is a union contract or other agreement to the contrary. If an employer chooses to pay you during some part of the leave, he is under no obligation to pay for the rest of the leave time allowed by law. You may choose or an employer may require that you use sick leave, vacation leave or any personal days first. Those days will count toward the 12 weeks you are permitted. If the employer does not normally pay for sick time, he does not need to under this law.

An eligible employee is entitled to a total of 12 workweeks of leave during any 12 month period for one or more of the following reasons:

- The birth of the employee's child (The leave is valid for 12 months only)
- To care for the employee's new born child
- The placement with the employee of a child for adoption or foster care
- To care for a spouse, son, daughter, or parent if that person has a serious health condition
  - A serious health condition is an illness, injury, impairment, or physical or mental condition that involves
    - In-patient care in a hospital, hospice, or residential medical care facility or
    - continuing treatment by a health care provider

- Because of a serious health condition that makes the employee unable to perform the functions of the position.

If your spouse is employed by the same employer, the 12 week total leave entitlement is a total for both parties combines. You are not entitled to 12 weeks each. An employer is never prohibited from providing more than the law allows. These are minimum entitlements.

Intermittent Leave

If you wish to take the leave on an intermittent basis, that is, not all at once, you and your employer must agree or if medically necessary. If leave is taken on an intermittent basis, it shall not affect the total amount of leave for which you are eligible.

If you request a leave for a foreseeable event, such as a planned medical treatment, the employer may require you to transfer temporarily to another job for which you are qualified, and that has equivalent pay and benefits, when that other job lends itself better to the leave.

Advance notice

When the leave is foreseeable, as in an expected birth, you need to give at least 30 days' notice, when practical and possible, before the leave begins. When possible, you must make a reasonable effort to not disrupt the operations of the employer.

Certification

An employer may require that the need for a leave be certified by an appropriate health care provider. The certificate is sufficient if it indicates that the employee is needed to care for a son, daughter, spouse, or parent and states all of the following:

- The date the condition began
- The expected duration of the condition the amount of time the employee will be needed to provide the care
- The appropriate medical facts which justify the request

If the leave is intermittent, the date and duration of the specific treatment requiring the short term leave should also be indicated as well as the fact that the leave will assist in the patient's recovery.

If the employer has any reason to doubt the validity of the certification, he may require, at his expense, a second opinion by another health care provider. He may not, however, select a provider who is regularly employed by him.

If the second opinion does not agree with the first opinion, the employer may, at his own expense, require a third opinion from a health care provider designated or approved jointly by employer and employee. The third opinion is binding on both parties.

The employer may periodically require recertification on a reasonable basis.

Restoration to position

An employee may return from a leave and must be restored to the same position as when the leave started or to an equivalent position with equivalent benefits, pay and terms of employment. The leave cannot result in the loss of any benefits. However, the employer does not need to count or award seniority or other employment benefits during the period of leave.

An employer may require a medical certificate before allowing the employee to return to work. The employer may also require the employee to report periodically on the progress of the patient.

If a contract is in effect or if there is a local or state law governing the return to work of an employee, this law shall not negate that rule or law.

Exemption to Leave

An employer may deny restoring an employee following a leave if:

- Restoring the employee would cause substantial and grievous economic injury to the employer
- The employer notifies the employee that restoration will be denied (This notice must be made as soon as the employer determines that the economic injury will occur)
- After the leave has started, the employee elects not to return to employment after receiving this notice

Affected by this paragraph are salaried employees among the highest paid 10 percent of the employees working within 75 miles of the facility.

Health benefits

During a leave, the employer must maintain coverage under his group health plan under the same conditions as if the employee were still working. However, the employer is entitled to recover any premiums paid during the leave if the employee does not return to work after the leave period or if the employee does not return to work for any reason other than the continuation, recurrence or onset of a serious health condition with entitles the employee to a leave. Also exempt from this section are circumstances beyond the control of the employee. An employer may require certification as in the original instance and the employee must provide that certificate promptly.

The certificate is sufficient if it states that a serious health condition prevented the employee from being able to perform the functions of her position on the date the leave time expired. It will also be deemed sufficient if the certificate states that the employee is needed to care for the child, spouse, or parent who has a serious health condition on the date the leave expired.

Legal recourse

An employer who violates this law shall be liable for damages equal to the amount of any wages, benefits or other compensation denied or lost because of a violation of this law. In a case where the employee does not lose any compensation, she may recover:

- Any actual monetary losses sustained as a direct result of the violation, such as the cost of providing care, up to a sum equal to 12 weeks of the employee's wages or salary
- Interest on the above amount at the prevailing rate
- Liquidated damages equal to the total amount above
- Reasonable attorney fees, witness fees, and other costs associated with the action

A judge may adjust that amount if the judge feels that the employer acted in good faith and had reasonable grounds to believe he had not committed a violation. A suit under this paragraph may be instituted in any Federal or State court and against any employer, including a public agency.

The right to sue ends if the Secretary of Labor files an action either on your behalf or independently. You may again sue if the court dismisses the Secretary's suit without prejudice.

Any suit under this section must be filed within two years of the date of the last event of the alleged violation. If the violation is willful, action may be brought for three years. The date which determines the two or three year requirement is the date the suit is filed.

Educational Agency Employees

Special rules apply to employees of any local educational agency, any private elementary or secondary school. If the employee needs a leave for more than 20 percent of the working days of the year, the agency or school may require that the employee:

- Take a leave for a particular period of time
- Transfer to another temporary position for which the employee is qualified that has
  - Equivalent pay and benefits and
  - Is better able to accommodate the leave

If a teacher begins a leave more than five weeks prior to the end of the academic term, the school may require that the teacher continue on leave until the end of the term if the leave is expected to last at least three weeks, and if the teacher's return would occur during the last three weeks of the term.

If a teacher begins a leave less than five weeks from the end of a term, the school may require the leave to continue to the end of the term if the leave is at least two weeks and would end during the final two weeks of the term.

For a leave beginning within three weeks of the end of the term, the school may require the leave to continue to the end of the term if the leave would be for at least five working days.

The restoration of a teacher to her position shall be governed by school board policy or practices or by collective bargaining agreements.

Civil Service Employees

For this section, an employee must be employed for at least 12 months in a permanent position. District of Columbia local government employees are not covered. The rules are the same as for other covered employees (other than teachers) except for the following: The condition for a leave includes an inability to perform the functions of the job, caused by a serious health condition. Intermittent leave or reduced work hours requires the agreement of both the employee and the agency and the leave period can be computed on an hour by hour basis.

If the agency agrees to an intermittent leave or reduced hours, they may require that the employee transfer to an alternative position. The employee may elect to use accrued sick leave or vacation time.

Wherever possible, the employee must give at least 30 days notice. The employee should try to schedule any treatment so as not to disrupt unduly the operations of the agency.

Appendix E - Funeral Checklist

Although you can and should allow family and friends to help, it is important to plan ahead so that you are not faced with the daunting task of making arrangements at the worst possible time. Use this checklist to make sure nothing is forgotten or ignored. You should update this list whenever you move or when any significant change occurs. For instance, the birth of a grandchild or wishes for cremation rather than the standard burial previously indicated.

To make it as easy as possible, copy the form on the following pages and keep it in a place where you can get to it when needed. This will also remind you to discuss some of these issues with the patient.

If the patient is in a facility, ask the staff which of these items they will take care of.

Some of the information may appear more than once but it will be more easily located when you need it.

FUNERAL CHECKLIST

(Attach a separate piece of paper wherever necessary)
Notifications:
Doctor: Name: ....

Phone: ....

Coroner: ....

Phone: ....
Ask the doctor if you need to make this call.

Funeral Home: ....

Director: ....

Address: ....

City: ....

Phone: ....
The funeral director should assist by coordinating with the cemetery, social security issues, securing the needed number of death certificates, and with many of the arrangements listed in this form.

Clergy: Name: ....

Phone: ....

Place of Worship: ....

Address: ....

City: .... State: ....

Spouse: ....

Phone: ....

Children:

.... Phone: ....

.... Phone: ....

.... Phone: ....

.... Phone: ....

Siblings:

.... Phone: ....

.... Phone: ....

.... Phone: ....

Friends:

.... Phone: ....

.... Phone: ....

.... Phone: ....

.... Phone: ....

Business Associates:

.... Phone: ....

.... Phone: ....

.... Phone: ....

Pallbearers:

....

....

....

....

Insurance:

Company: ....

Agent: ....

Phone: ....

Company: ....

Agent: ....

Phone: ....

Banks:

Name: ....

Phone: ....

Account No.: ....

Name: ....

Phone: ....

Account No.: ....

Florist: ....

Phone: ....

Organist: ....

     Phone: ....

Soloist: ....

     Phone: ....

Speakers:

     Name: ....

        Phone: ....

     Name: ....

        Phone: ....

Organ Donation:

    ❑ Any needed organ or body part

    ❑ No donation

    ❑ Specific organs only (specify)

       ....

       ....

       ....

Location of Living Will:

    ....

Location of Last Will and Testament:

    ....

Safe Deposit Box:

    Location: ....

       Box no.: ....

       Location of Key: ....

Executor of estate: ....

    The Funeral Home will assist with the following:

Cemetery:

       Name: ....

       Address: ....

       City, State: ....

       Plot no.: ....

Service location:
- ❑ Place of worship
- ❑ Funeral Home
- ❑ Graveside

Casket style or number: ....
(You are not required to purchase the casket from the funeral home. If you have purchased one independently, enter the following:)

       Casket company: ....

       Contract number: ....

       Phone ....

Burial clothing (include jewelry if desired):

....

....

....

....

Readings:

....

....

....

....

Preferred music:

....

....

....

....

Vital statistics (will also be used for newspaper notices):

Full name (maiden):
....

Address:

....

City, state: ....

Former city, state: ....

Date of birth: ....

Place of birth: ....

Social security no. (not for newspaper):

.... - .... - ....

Veteran's discharge or claim no.:

....

Father's name:

....

Mother's name (with maiden):

....

Marriage date and place:

....

Spouse name (with maiden):

....
Note if any of the above is deceased

Children:

Name: ....

Spouse: ....

City/State: ....

Name: ....

    Spouse: ....

    City/State: ....

Name: ....

    Spouse: ....

    City/State: ....

Name: ....

    Spouse: ....

    City/State: ....

Grandchildren:

Name: ....

    Spouse: ....

    City/State: ....

Name: ....

    Spouse: ....

    City/State: ....

Name: ....

    Spouse: ....

    City/State: ....

Name: ....

    Spouse: ....

City/State: ....

Name: ....

Spouse: ....

City/State: ....

Name: ....

Spouse: ....

City/State: ....

Other survivors (include relationship if appropriate):

Name: ....

City/State: ....

Name: ....

City/State: ....

Name: ....

City/State: ....

Education:

School: ....

Degree: ....

School: ....

Degree: ....

School: ....

Degree: ....

Military Service:

Branch: ....

Years: ....

Awards or honors:

....

Most recent occupation (list more than one if you wish):

....

....

Notable achievements or awards:

....

....

Memberships (organizations, unions):

....

....

....

Visiting hours:

Location: ....

Day : .... Date: .... Times: ....

Day : .... Date: .... Times: ....

Day : .... Date: .... Times: ....
Funeral Service:

Location: ....

Day : .... Date: .... Time: ....
Burial:

Cemetery: ....

Location: ....

Remembrances:
❑ Flowers   ❑ No Flowers
❑ Contributions to:

....

....

Reminders:
Pick up from the airport:

....

....

Rides to funeral and cemetery:

....

....

Hotel arrangements:

Thank you notes:

Appendix F - Airline Rules

This listing is limited to airlines flying **domestic routes** within the United States.[37] We do not list those which are commuter lines only. No effort has been made to include all airlines in the world. Airlines constantly merge, dissolve, restructure and come into being. Check with the airline to be sure these rules have not changed and that the airline is still in existence. Also, remember that all special arrangements take more time at the airport. Especially with the increased security now

---

[37] We have not included airlines who fly between the US and foreign destinations exclusively. Although most international carriers will have similar rules, we suggest you check with the airlines, including connecting airlines, before booking international flights.

required, allow enough extra time to discuss your needs with everyone at the airport.

As the result of FAA rules, those airlines which allow **oxygen concentrators** limit the selection to AirSep Freestyle and Lifestyle models, Imogen One, Respironics EverGo and SeQual Eclipse devices only. In many cases, these units need to be modified for air travel. You should also have extra batteries with you.

Supplemental oxygen requirements are dictated by the Federal Aviation Administration and allow its use during flight only. It will be turned off during take-offs, landings, and while taxiing. Medical certification is required.

All **medications** should be carried on, not placed in luggage.

Wheelchairs are available at virtually all airports and from all airlines. Discuss your needs with each airline when you make the reservations. Many carriers will also have **electric carts** available.

Service animals are always allowed according to FAA rules. The primary restriction is that the animal must not obstruct the aisle.

If your patient is **traveling alone**, but you are helping them, passes are available so you can go to the gate, even though you are not flying with the patient. Discuss your needs with the ticket agent.

All airlines offer **early boarding** when needed.

There are many other rules which indicate requirements for various flights depending upon the number of seats, number of aisles, or when the aircraft was manufactured. They include wheelchair accessible lavatories, move-able arm rests, and on-board wheelchairs. If your equipment requires batteries, you may not use liquid, only dry cell batteries.

Other FAA rules dictate that assistive devices are not counted toward carry-on luggage limits. Also, the typical luggage liabilities do not apply to assistive devices. Don't ever sign a waiver. The airline may require 48 hour notice for any assistive service you may require.

Many items may be available depending upon the specific airplane which will be used on the flight. These include provisions for the use of oxygen or respirators which are tied in to the aircraft power (adaptors may be required), stretchers, electric wheelchairs, and a lift if there is no jetway to the particular aircraft.

The rules and conditions cited in this section may not include every requirement or availability from every airline. Check with the carrier in all cases.

Most airlines offer **bereavement fares**. Ask your carriers.

- Air Midwest Airlines www.mesa-air.com
  602-685-4000
  - Regional service with major airlines
- Air Tran   www.airtran.com
  800-247-8726
  - Allows oxygen concentrator
    - Passenger form on-line
  - No supplemental oxygen
  - No stretcher service
  - No medical equipment requiring aircraft electrical power
  - Electric carts acceptable (in place of wheelchair)
  - On-board wheelchair available
- Air Wisconsin   See US Airways
  - Operates as US Airways Express
  - Also operates as United Express
- Alaska   Airlines   www.alaskaair.com
  800-252-7522
  - Allows oxygen concentrators
    - $50 fee
  - Supplemental oxygen available
    - One-way fees range up to $350
    - Available on flight numbers up to 999 only

- o Peanut and other allergies must be disclosed
  - When making reservation, ask for a *peanut buffer zone*
  - Remind the attendant at check-in
  - Remind the flight attendant on the plane
- o No refrigeration available for medicines which must be kept cool
- o Stretcher service only between Alaska and either Seattle, WA or Portland, OR; and within the state of Alaska
  - 24 hour advance notice required
  - Other restrictions and fees apply
- America West
  - o Allows oxygen concentrator
    - Inform gate attendant
- American Airlines   www.aa.com
  800-433-7300
  - o Allows oxygen concentrator
    - Must fit under the seat
  - o Supplemental oxygen available
    - Consult airline for charges
  - o No refrigeration available
  - o No precautions for allergies
  - o Braille safety cards
- American Eagle   See American Airlines
  - o No supplementary oxygen
- Atlantic Southeast Airlines
                    See Skywest Airlines
- Big Sky Airlines   See Delta Airlines
  - o Operates as Delta Connection
  - o Shares codes with US Air, Northwest, Alaska Air and Hawaiian Airlines
- Chautauqua Airlines
                    See Republic Airways
  - o Regional carrier flying under various names
- Colgan Airlines   See major carrier

- o Operates as Continental Connection, US Air Express, and United Express
- Comair   See Delta Airlines
  - o Operates as Delta Connection
  - o Allows oxygen concentrator
  - o No supplemental oxygen
- Continental Airlines
                    www.Continental.com
  800-932-2732
  - o Allows oxygen concentrator
  - o Supplemental oxygen available
    - Medical release forms available on-line
    - Advance notice with return phone call
    - Consult oxygen desk for charges
  - o No refrigeration available
  - o Allows electric cart (in place of wheelchair)
- Delta Airlines   www.Delta.com
  800-221-1212
  - o Allows oxygen concentrator
    - Advance notice with return phone call
    - $25 fee per itinerary
  - o Supplemental oxygen available
    - $100 fee per flight
    - 48 hour advance notice with return phone call
  - o No refrigeration available
  - o Peanut buffer zone available
- Delta Connection   See Delta Airlines
  - o No supplemental oxygen
- Delta Shuttle   See Delta Airlines
  - o No supplemental oxygen
- Express Jet   www.xjet.com
  888-958-9538
  - o Some flights under Continental Express and Delta Connections
  - o Allows oxygen concentrator
  - o No supplemental oxygen

- o No onboard wheelchairs available
- Frontier Airlines
  www.frontierairlines.com
  800-432-1359
  - o Allows oxygen concentrator
  - o No supplementary oxygen
  - o Medical authorization available on-line
- Great Lakes Airlines
  www.FlyGreatLakes.com
  800-554-5111
  - o Regional carrier
  - o Shares codes with Frontier and United
  - o Smaller, propeller driven planes only
  - o Contact airline for allowable items
- Hawaiian Airlines
  www.Hawaiianair.com
  800-367-5320
  - o Allows oxygen concentrator
  - o No supplemental oxygen except within the state of Hawaii
- Horizon Air   See Alaska Air
  - o Allows oxygen concentrator
    - $50 fee
  - o No supplemental oxygen
  - o Peanut and other allergies must be disclosed
    - When making reservation, ask for a *peanut buffer zone*
    - Remind the attendant at check-in
    - Remind the flight attendant on the plane
  - o No refrigeration available
- Jet Blue Airways   www.jetblue.com
  800-538-2583
  - o Contact airline for allowable items
- Mesa Airlines   www.mesa-air.com
  602-685-4000
  - o Regional airline under major carriers

- Mesaba Airlines   See Northwest Airlines
  - Adult assistance program
    - See Northwest for details
- Midwest Airlines
              www.midwestairlines.com
        800-452-2022
  - Allows oxygen concentrator
  - On-board wheelchair
  - Allows ventilators
  - Allows respirators
- Northwest Airlines   www.nwa.com
        800-225-2525
  - Supplemental oxygen available
  - Stretcher service available
    - Medical certificate required
  - Adult assistance program
    - Dedicated personal attention door-to-door
    - $50 fee if non-stop
    - $75 fee not non-stop
    - Includes transfer, layovers and connections
    - No medication services
    - Not available on some flights
- Piedmont Airlines   See US Airways
  - Wholly owned subsidiary of US Airways
  - Operates as US Air Express
- Pinnacle Airline   See Northwest Airlines
  - Adult assistance program
    - See Northwest for details
- PSA Airlines   See US Airways
  - Wholly owned subsidiary of US Airways
  - Operates as US Air Express
- Republic Airways   www.rjet.com
        317-484-4000
  - Regional carrier group flying under several companies
- Shuttle America   See Republic Airways
  - Regional carrier flying under several companies

- Skywest Airlines   www.skywest.com
  - Operates as Delta Connection, United Express, and Midwest Connect
  - Also operates Atlantic Southeast Airlines
  - No supplementary oxygen
  - Check major carrier for other details
- Southwest Airlines www.Southwest.com 800-435-9792
  - Allows oxygen concentrator
  - No supplemental oxygen
  - Peanut allergy travelers must alert agents
    - Will not serve peanuts on such flights
      - No guarantee because of peanut dust
- Spirit Airlines   www.spiritair.com 800-772-7117
  - No oxygen
  - On-board wheelchair
- Ted   ww.United.com 800-864-8331
  - Part of United Airlines
- Trans States Airlines   See major airline
  - Regional carrier for United Airlines, American Airlines, and US Airways
- United Airlines   www.United.com 800-864-8331
  - Oxygen concentrators not allowed
  - Supplemental oxygen available
    - Medical certificate available on-line
    - Fee required but not indicated
- United Express   see United Airlines
  - No oxygen service
- US Airways   www.usairways.com 800-428-4322
  - Allows oxygen concentrators
    - Inform gate agent
  - Peanut buffer zone not available

- US Airways Express   See US Airways
  - o Operates Air Wisconsin
- USA 3000 Airlines   www.USA3000.com
    877-872-3000
  - o Allows portable ventilators
  - o Allows portable respirators
  - o No oxygen, except in on-board emergencies
  - o Domestic service between Florida only and other cities

Appendix G - Oxygen Suppliers

This is not meant to be a complete list of suppliers. There are many suppliers who are local or regional suppliers only. Consult with the hospital and your doctor for other companies in your area.

- All Medical Sales and Rentals, Inc.
  - www.portableoxygenman.com
    - 888-280-2677
- CPR Savers & First Aid Supply
  - www.cpr-savers.com
    - 800-480-1277
- DealMed Medical Supplies
  - www.dealmed.com
    - 800-569-0570
- E/Pax
  - www.emergencypax.com
    - 888-416-9257
- Home Fill
  - www.myhomefill.com
    - 866-806-5544

- Jazzy Electric Wheelchairs
  - www.jazzy-electric-wheelchairs.com
    - 800-790-5523
- Lincare Inc.
  - www.lincare.com
    - 727-530-7900
- Medical Supplies 4 Less
  - www.medical-supplies-4-less.com
    - 800-470-8856
- Oxygen To Go
  - www.oxygentogo.com
    - 877-736-8691
- Specialty Medical Supply
  - www.specialtymedicalsupply.com
    - 800-380-8539
- Vitality Medical
  - www.vitalitymedical.com
    - 800-397-5899

Appendix H - Medication Checklist

On the following page is a medication checklist for you to follow. Keep the original on your refrigerator with either a magnet or tape.

For every medical appointment, take a copy with you.

Keep the list up to date and make changes as soon as a doctor changes the instructions.

You can review the list with the pharmacist as often as you feel necessary.

Appendix H - Medication Checklist

Keep this chart on your refrigerator and be sure to take a copy with you to each medical appointment. In addition, ask your pharmacist to examine the list for any possible interactions.

Medication	Prescribed By	Strength	Reason Taken	When? am/pm	Start Date	Qty	Stop Date	Notes

Appendix J - Test Record

Depending upon the patient's age, condition, or problems, not all tests may be indicated or advisable. Some my be performed regularly, others annually, still others only once or if indications change. Consult with the doctor.

This chart should be kept updated at all times. You can also bring the chart with you to all medical appointments so you can review it as necessary with the doctor.

Appendix J - Test Record

Test	How Often	Doctor	Date Taken	Notes
Blood Pressure				
Bone Density				
Cholesterol				
Colorectal				
Dental				
Hearing				
Mammography				

Appendix J - Test Record

Test	How Often	Doctor	Date Taken	Notes
Pap Smear				
Prostrate				
Sugar				
Tuberculosis				
Vision				
Weight				

Appendix J - Test Record

Immunizations	How Often	Doctor	Date Taken	Notes
Flu				
Tetanus/ Diptheria	every 10 years			
Hepatitis B				
Measles/Mumps/ Rubela	at least once			
Pneumonia	at age 65			

Index

Hepatitis B 31
Herbal
   Supplements...87
HIPAA.................13
HMO...................33
Hoarseness.........80
Home Health Care
   ....29, 30, 32
Home Safety .40, 51
Homeopathic 76
Homeowners
   Insurance .20, 28
Hormone 82
Hospice .18, 29, 58,
   98, 100, 169
Hospital. 18, 51, 59,
   74, 76, 98, 99
   Beds 31
   Bills 38, 39
   Concerns 62
   Meals.............29
   Private Room ..29
   Rooms 29
   Services ...14, 29,
   102
   Supplies..........29
   Support Groups
  63
Housekeeping...... 6
Hygiene 93
Hyperactivity 113
Identification
   Bracelet 94
Implants.............77
In Hospital.........29
Income 37
Income Tax.........21
Independent Living
  38
Infant 16
Informed Consent
   ....75, 103

In-Home
   Air Conditioning6
   Care 5
   Cleanliness....... 6
   Food 7
   Fuel................. 6
   Furnace........... 5
   Heat 6
   Housekeeping... 6
   Locks 6
   Plumbing.......... 6
   Refrigerator 7
   Smoke Detectors
   7
   Telephone......... 6
Injury................ 76
In-Patient 2, 17, 29,
   112, 169
Insulin ... 31, 32, 91
Insurance.... 12, 24,
   26, 28, 38, 59,
   60, 63, 71, 114,
   132, 161
   Coverage 19, 101,
   102, 112, 134
   Health20, 21, 28,
   99
   Homeowners.. 20,
   28
   Incidental Office
   28
   Life................ 20
   Nursing Home
   106
   Plans........... 115
Intercom 57
Interns............ 101
Intervention 17
Irritability.......... 93
IV 29
Job Security..... 168
Kidney Dialysis .. 31

Upcoming books from
Rosstrum Publishing

Fast Track for Parents: By Esther Ross and Joseph Ross. On the heels of Fast Track for Caregivers, parents will gain answers to important questions on rearing children, especially those with disabilities.

Fast Track to the Right Job: By Dale Phillips. Learn how to improve the skills you need to find and land the job you want. Gain the information you need to successfully win the right job. Find tips to succeed and things to avoid, from the resume to the interview.

Fiction:

Lawless in Brazil: By Mike Johnson. A young boy hires part time bartender and private eye Jake Lawless to find his missing mother. The trail leads Lawless to Brazil, international intrigue and danger at every turn.

Timberline: By Bernie Ziegner. An airliner crashes in the western mountains of Montana. Tom Bauer rescues a woman from the wreckage, unaware of the cargo on the plane. Mob threats and violence threaten Bauer and all he holds dear. Timberline is a place where the frontier can still be found and dreams can still come true.

To receive advance notification of upcoming publications, send your e-mail address with your request to:
RosstrumPublishing@gmail.com

www.ingramcontent.com/pod-product-compliance
Lightning Source LLC
Chambersburg PA
CBHW020511100426
42813CB00030B/3194/J